Survival of the Fittest

ATTITUDES

SKILLS

BEHAVIORS

Survival of the Fittest

How the Future of Union Construction Depends on Every Journeyman, Every Apprentice and You

Mark Breslin

McALLY
INTERNATIONAL
PRESS
SAN RAMON, CALIFORNIA

11th printing 2008

ISBN-13: 978-0-9741662-4-7
ISBN-10: 0-9741662-4-3
LCCN: 2005927100

Contents

v

CHAPTER 6
Personal Responsibility 59

CHAPTER 7
Work Ethic, Commitment, and Attitude . . 69

■ Back in the Classroom
■ The Training Center—What a Deal
■ The Training Staff
■ Steel, Iron, Wood…and Microchips?
■ Big Companies vs. Small Companies

■ Being Financially Responsible
■ Credit Cards: The Bottomless Pit
■ In Over Your Head
■ Little Things Add Up
■ Million Dollar Blue Collar

■ For Foremen Only
■ The Money Maker
■ Leading by Example
■ The Mentor and Coach
■ The Paperwork King
■ The Yelling Idiot
■ A Professional, Not a Pal
■ The Foreman Who Plays Favorites
■ Ten Tips for Being a Great Foreman
■ Ten Tips for Being a Lousy Foreman

■ An Invitation to Leadership
■ Be a Mentor
■ Passing it Along: The Vanishing Craft Masters
■ Moving up in Your Union
■ Steward
■ Red, White, and Blue Collar Voter

Introduction

My family has been in the construction business for close to 100 years. I've followed in the footsteps of my great grandfather, grandfather, and dad; all contractors and craftsmen. I have learned about accomplishment, leadership, and responsibility and I have paid for these lessons. I've also had plenty of luck along the way and moved up in the world further than I ever could have imagined.

Now I'm trying to give something back. I am trying to inspire and help others to go further than they can imagine. That's the main thing I hope you'll get from reading this book. My family history is rooted in the grit and challenge of the job site, and that's the tone I've put into this book. It is a book written for you, in your language. And though I use the term "guy" throughout, it is for every man and woman who will serve the union construction industry.

The advice I have to give is based on my experiences both on and off the job. Not all the lessons are easy; in fact, most of them aren't. This business can be tough, but the rewards of accomplishment, pride, and financial security are worth it.

Now I know some guys don't like change and will do anything to avoid it. If you're one of those guys, you're probably not going to like this book very much. So I apologize in advance for any offense taken by anyone who isn't ready, willing, and able to join in the fight for union construction.

On the other hand, if you are offended, tough shit.

Mark Breslin

Who is this book for?

This book was written for, and is dedicated to, every member of every construction union in the United States and Canada. Every rank and file member of the following organizations deserves to compete and succeed as the best in the world:

- Laborers International Union of North America
- International Brotherhood of Electrical Workers
- International Union of Operating Engineers
- United Brotherhood of Carpenters and Joiners of America
- International Union of Bricklayers & Allied Craftsmen
- International Association of Bridge, Structural, Ornamental and Reinforcing Ironworkers
- Sheet Metal Workers International Union
- United Association of US and Canada
- International Association of Operative Plasterers & Cement Masons
- International Union of Elevator Constructors
- International Association of Heat & Frost Insulators & Asbestos Workers
- International Brotherhood of Boilermakers
- International Brotherhood of Teamsters
- United Union of Roofers, Waterproofers and Allied Workers
- International Union of Painters and Allied Trades
- All other unions engaged in construction and industrial work in North America

It's also for the tens of thousands of union contractors and the hundreds of associations in partnership with each of these unions, employing more than 2 million craft workers.

What is this book about?

1. It's about being a success at your job and in your life.
2. It's about union construction taking back the marketplace.
3. It's about how #1 and #2 directly relate to each other.

Where does it apply?

It applies anyplace where union construction is committed to being the most productive, the highest quality, and the best value in the world—on every job site, every day.

Why write this book?

This book was written for three reasons:

1. Because union construction is having a tough time competing.
2. Because union construction is worth saving.
3. Because you deserve to be successful and live the best life possible.

HOW many excuses can I come up with not to read this book?

How about I help you with the first ten:

1. I hate to read.
2. I already know everything I need to know about my job.
3. I can already tell it's a bunch of bullshit.
4. Two words: *Baywatch* re-runs.
5. Not enough pictures.
6. Monday Night Football!
7. Somebody tricked me into learning something once, and that's not going to happen again.
8. Somebody's making me read it and I hate that.
9. It's already boring.
10. I'll just wait for it to come out on DVD.

When will this book matter to me?

Every single day of your life.

Survival of the Fittest

"Labor cannot stand still. It must not retreat.
It must go on, or go under."

Harry Bridges

This book is about a fight for survival. On the front lines are the more than 2 million union construction workers and contractors working in North America today, fighting together for the marketplace. If you haven't seen the fight yet, you will, and soon. In fact, like it or not, you're destined to become part of it.

The fight is called *Survival of the Fittest*, and what it means is simple: if you're the most adaptable and determined, you will survive. If you're not, you won't. It's the law of the jungle and the street, and it's the way of the world we live in. Has been for millions of years. You don't need to watch *Animal Planet* to figure it out. Any living thing—plant or animal—that's not the best adapted to its environment gets eaten up, is pushed out, or just plain dies off and goes extinct. It's exactly the same in the construction industry. If we can't adapt to our environment, or if we can't compete in a changing industry, we'll be eliminated.

Our Fight and Challenge

In our industry, there's a battle raging between union and non-union construction. Today, *less than 15 percent of the construction work in North America is union.* Which means more than 85 percent is now non-union. And these numbers are barely holding.

Thirty years ago it was the other way around. Back then, unions had the lion's share of the work in the United States and Canada. Today they do a fraction of what they used to. More than 80 percent of the work is non-union. That's eight-out-of-ten workers, and eight-out-of-ten job sites.

How did it happen? Everybody put their heads in the sand and pretended it wasn't happening, that's how. The truth is this: union construction has gotten its' ass kicked for the past 30 years, all across this country, and Canada, too. Sure, there are still pockets like New York, San Francisco, Chicago, and St. Louis—but for most of the country, non-union is the rule, not the exception, and that makes us the underdog. And when you're the underdog, you have to work harder. A lot harder.

Here's What Happened and What We're Going to DO About It

Over time, for various reasons, owners, developers, and everybody else who used to use only union contractors and workers decided they didn't need us anymore. And like it or not, a lot of it was our fault. We took things for granted. When things are good, it's easy to think it will *always* be that way. Just ask the next dinosaur you see. We had the market, but we let it get away. We didn't see the changes coming, or if we did, we tried to ignore them.

Can we take back the market? Hell yes. What's it going to take? Each one of us (as members of *The Fittest*) is going to have to take back our place at the top. We have to rise up and compete like never before. And if you think you can just wait it out, believe me, pretty soon there won't be anything left to wait for. If you don't want to make the hard choices now, they'll be made for you.

It's not like you have to go it alone. If we all do what we need to do, we'll have a couple of million union workers and contractors in North America, and that's an army to be reckoned with. Every union guy who ever pounded nails, poured concrete, or tied re-bar. Every blue collar who's welded, flagged traffic, pulled wire, walked a beam, raked asphalt, or set a turbine. Guys who lay flooring or mop roofs or move dirt. Truck drivers, pipe liners, framers, painters, plasterers, and mechanics. All the above are facing the same challenge you are. It's a challenge for every apprentice, every journeyman, and every foreman who holds a union card. A challenge for every one of you who will ever build union.

I know there'll be plenty of union guys who don't want hear about it. Some guys don't care as long as they still have a job and a check coming in every week. This is what's also known as the screw-everybody-I-got-mine approach. Just my opinion, but selfish bastards like that might not be the ones you want to listen to when you're thinking about your own future.

Anybody that *wants* to see *can* see that union construction across the entire U.S. and Canada has been losing ground every day, every month, every year since the 1960s. It's happened very slowly, and that's why it's been hard to see. We used to have the whole pie. Now we've got one slice left, and it's not even a big one.

The unions and the contractors are out there fighting to get a bigger slice of that pie again. They're talking to owners, developers, and builders about how it's worth paying top dollar for union construction because it's a better value. But they can only do so much. It's up to every rank and file member to "put the walk behind the talk" by making union construction a better value on the job site every day. This starts with you and your crew.

If we're going to pull it off, if we're going to compete and win, every one of us needs to be a winner in every way. This book is about you being that winner, on the job site and in your life. It's not about living from dispatch to dispatch. It's not about building for "union pride" or because your boss says you have to. It's about doing the right things on and off the job to guarantee *your* job and *your* future. It's about looking out for yourself and your family. When you do right for yourself in that way, you do right for the union. And you also do right for the next generation of union construction workers, which may even include your own kids. Union construction is a proud tradition and a worthwhile heritage. Do your part to keep it strong. Nobody's going to do it for us. It's our responsibility to ourselves, our unions, and our industry. Now's the time to show that we're the smartest and most adaptable to change. It's time to win. Every hour. Every day. On every job site.

Just remember, talk without action is bullshit.

You want the money?
You want the respect?
You want the future?

Let's go get it.

Chapter One The Truth Hurts

"The truth hurts. Maybe not as much
as jumping on a bicycle with a seat missing,
but it still hurts."

—from *Naked Gun 2* (The Movie)

The Truth Hurts

On an average day, across the United States and Canada, more than 2 million union construction workers put in 16 million hours. On that same day, between 10-and-12 million non-union construction workers work about 100 million hours. This is not a good thing.

Back in the day, union construction ruled. What happened? How did we get here? Well, change happened, and obviously not for the better. Change happens to all kinds of people, companies, and industries. Change happens to everybody all the time, whether we like it or not. How many times have you heard guys say, "well, I remember back in the good old days…" Newsflash: the "good old days" don't pay the bills anymore.

We don't like change, especially when things are fine just the way they are. Unfortunately, it's not up to us. For example:

- On my old 4x4, I had to turn the hubs, not press a button
- I used to watch TV without cable, and dishes were things you ate food off of
- I used to buy eight-track tapes. Then I bought cassettes. Now it's an *iPod*
- Banking? Shopping? Entertainment? Games? Research? Travel? All now on the Internet.
- Yard sale vs. E-Bay
- What did guys do before Viagra? (Hold on another minute honey…)

Face it, change happens whether we like it or not. And that is the truth. And yes, sometimes it hurts.

Change Takes No Prisoners: Dead Brands

What do these companies have in common?

- Oldsmobile
- Pan Am Airlines
- Consolidated Freight
- U.S. Steel
- Montgomery Ward.

Not long ago, all these companies were successful in the marketplace. Now they don't even exist. They all went broke. They've all been replaced by somebody else.

What's the point? Companies that used to be on top got killed in the marketplace because they didn't change fast enough. It's the same with us. Just because we've been competitive in the past is no guarantee that tomorrow the marketplace won't throw our asses out.

Over the years, the ones that die before their time are the ones that would not or could not change fast enough. So for union construction to say we don't have to change with the times is just plain crazy. For us to think we can just keep doing business like it's 1960—or even 1980—makes no sense. The world around us is different, and that means we have to be different.

When the last Oldsmobile rolled off the line, I bet the guys in charge were wondering what the hell happened. They'd probably looked around a couple of decades earlier and said, "Well, our cars aren't selling quite as well as they used to, but we're still doing OK. Anyway, it's probably just temporary; things will probably get back to normal in a few years." So they didn't bother changing. They just kept making ugly, boxy cars right up till the end. In denial. By the time they realized the market had changed for good, they were f--ked. They didn't think it could happen to them, but it did. Think it could happen to us? *It already did.*

Dinosaurs, the Buffalo, Krispy Kremes, and YOU

The dinosaurs died out. Most of the buffalo got killed off. Krispy Kreme fired 25 percent of their workers when the Atkins diet hit. None of them ever saw it coming. Who'll get the ax next? Not us…if we start paying close attention and make the right choices.

Chapter Two

Survival of the Fittest and WIIFY

(What's In It For You?)

Performance Profile: Dale Earnhardt

Title of Profile: **The Intimidator**

Name: Dale Earnhardt

Profile: The most feared and respected competitor ever to drive on the NASCAR circuit.

Key to Success: Relentless, fearless, total domination attitude

Backed It Up: Seven-time NASCAR Winston Cup champion; four-time winner, International Race of Champions; ESPY Driver of the Decade; Seven-time winner, Goody's 300 Busch series; five-time NMPA Driver of the Year.

Lesson: Incredible performance comes from accepting no excuses for not winning. Your competitor is just somebody who's in your way while you're in the process of winning.

WIIFY

Maybe you're thinking, who cares about change or being *The Fittest*? You're happy just being in the game. You're making decent bucks. You don't need to kill yourself, so why should you?

It's a valid point. Nobody does anything unless it's in their best interests, and you shouldn't be any different. It's how every one of us is wired. Bottom line: if we're going to act on something, there'd better be a payoff.

OK, then let's look at the payoff *for you*:

- Are you making all the money you want? Could you use a little more?
- Are your benefits as good as they could be? Want them to be better?
- Are your conditions on the job ideal?
- Would you like a shorter commute?
- Are you getting satisfaction from your work, or just putting in your hours?
- Are you really proud of who you are and what you do?
- Do you get all the hours you want every year?
- If you're an apprentice, are you worried about your future work prospects?

If you answered yes to any of these questions, keep reading.

Ninety Percent of the Pie:
What's In It For You?

We've got different percentages of the market in different places. And the reality in New York or Chicago is not the same as it is in Dallas or Phoenix. But when you average it out, we still only have around 13 percent of the work nationwide.

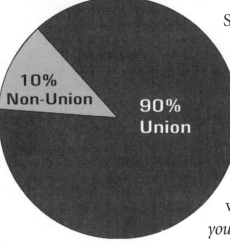

So let's wish a little. What would be different for you if we had 90 percent of the pie? What would it be like if we had 90 percent of the market and non-union workers had to get by on the other 10 percent? Who would benefit? Lets start with you. *What would be in it for you at 90 percent market share?*

Higher wages

Better health and welfare benefits

■ Full employment

■ More political influence

Better pension benefits

■ Better working conditions

More bargaining power

■ More money for training

■ Lower dues per month per member, but more union dues overall

■ More community support

Less commute travel to job sites

More even playing field for your contractors

■ Stable profits for your contractors

Control of the marketplace

More respect

You see why it's worth working on? We can have all these things if we work together to *grow the pie*. At less than 15 percent of the market, there's nothing left to give away. Every day, on every job site, we are either growing the pie or watching it shrink even more. And the pie grows or shrinks based on our skills, our attitudes, and our behaviors.

And by the way, there's one more thing you should know about the fight for survival: there's no tie game. We either win or lose.

Let's win.

What Else is in it for You? Ten New Pickups, or a Cabin, or an RV, a Boat, and four ATVs

In the construction industry, you're kind of in business for yourself. It might not seem that way, but it's true. Even if most people in the craft get paid the same hourly wages, you can bet that not everybody takes the same amount home at the end of each year.

Over 15 to 20 years, the way you work will determine your jobs, hours, and earnings. Is it a big deal? You bet it is. If you're really aiming to be the best craftsman at your hall, it'll come back in ways that you might not have thought about.

Let's just say that, because you have a great attitude and top skills, you end up getting an extra couple hundred hours a year—compared to the average guy—over your whole career. With a total hourly pay package of, say, $50, it adds up fast. If you figure 200 extra hours per year, times $50 per hour, times 30 years, that's a lot of extra cash right in your pocket.

200 hours x $50 per hour total package
x 30 years = *$300,000 in extra earnings*

So in case you were wondering what the difference is between a top hand and an average one, it's about three hundred grand. That's 10 new custom pick-ups, or a nice vacation cabin, or a custom RV, hot bass boat, and four ATVs. That's what is in it for you.

Chapter Three
Elite Warriors and Winners

"Winning starts with complete command
of the fundamentals. Then it takes desire,
determination, discipline and self-sacrifice."

—Jesse Owens

Individual Performance Profile:
Michael Jordan

Title of Profile: **Winning is Everything**

Name: Michael Jordan

Profile: Greatest player in basketball history

Key to Success: Total commitment to winning; motivating by example and getting the rest of his team to give their best.

Backed It Up: Six NBA titles. Five MVP titles. Ten scoring titles. Hall of Fame.

Lesson: Winning is a way of life. Motivating others to see this and act on it is how you get things done.

Winning: There's Nothing Like It

Have you ever competed in anything? Basketball? Baseball? Softball? Fishing? Racing? Skiing? Boxing? Marital arts? Poker? No matter what the game is, you probably like to compete. And if you like to compete, it goes without saying that you like to win. We humans are just competitive animals. It's in our nature to hunger to win.

Personally, I love to win. I want to win all the time. I hate losing. Losing sucks. Losing feels bad. Forget all that "it's how you play the game" stuff. That's bullshit. Whoever said that probably never won anything in his whole life. When you ask about last week's game, what's the first thing you want to know? You want to know who won, right? Even on my 11-year-old daughter's basketball team, they get pumped when they win. The reward of winning is what makes playing the game hard worth the effort in the first place.

Do you watch sports? Eighty million people watch the Super Bowl every year. More than a billion watch the Olympics. And about three billion people around the world are obsessed with soccer. What's it all about? Winning and losing. Competition. People driven to excel. People willing to train their entire lives, sometimes for a single shot at winning. Sweat, blood, pain, tears, joy, anger, and despair. Dreams made. Dreams crushed. Whether it's on an Olympic podium or on your job site, there's nothing in the world like the feeling of *winning*.

Team Performance Profile: Navy Seals

Title of Profile: **The Elite Warriors**

Name: U.S. NAVY SEALS

Profile: Premier special operations and counter-terrorism military organization in the world.

Key to Success: Only the elite belong on the team. Eighty percent dropout rate during training. They call it Hell Week for a reason. Setting the bar for the team as high as it can go. Total team commitment to the most lethal missions on earth.

Backed it up: First ones in, last ones out, on the most dangerous assignments around the globe.

Lesson: An elite team performs to where the bar is set—everyone, all the time. There is no compromise. Either you belong or you don't.

Navy SEALS, Setting the Bar, and You

Winning teams come in all different stripes. And uniforms. For example, let's look at the Navy SEALS and the National Guard. Both are branches of our country's military. So what's the difference? Only this: the skills, attitudes, and behavior required for success. Both require discipline, focus, and commitment, but for the SEALS the bar is set high. Very, very, high.

More than 80 percent of the guys that apply to become SEALS quit during training. That's because that ultra-high performance bar is out of their reach. They don't kick you out of SEAL training. You ring a bell, take off your helmet and walk away. You quit, because you found out that you don't belong. The bar was set for the organization, and you could not reach it. And let's face it; even the guys who wash out are probably hardcore to begin with. But even that's not enough. The ones who make it are totally committed to being the best of the best. They want to be something special. They want the pride that comes from being the most elite warriors in the world.

So what does this have to do with your job? Let's ask the hard questions:

■ How high is the performance bar set for you?

■ How high is it set for your fellow workers on the job site?

■ How many guys on the job aren't reaching that performance bar?

■ How many in your union aren't reaching it?

■ Do you put up with weak performers on the job?

■ Is the bar adjustable in the fight for Survival of the Fittest?

Being the best is not for everybody, and that's OK. But if you're not sure about the level of commitment you're willing to make, you should think about it long and hard. Union construction is supposed to be the best in the world. Not "good," not "above average," but *the best*. The thing is, the height of the bar is not just up to your foreman or superintendent; it's up to you. If you want to be an elite warrior in the fight for our marketplace, you need to set your own bar very high and expect it from everyone around you.

A Few Good Men
(and Some Not-So-Good Ones)

The Survival of the Fittest applies to every job site in North America. Elite warriors are there, along with guys who might not belong. The difference between the best, average, and just plain lousy can have a huge impact on where you fit and what you earn. After you've been around a while, you start to see the differences.

Let's take a look at a few categories on most job sites:

Elite Warriors: The Top Performers (5-10 percent)

The top 5-10 percent of rank-and-file field guys will have no worries most of the time they're in the union. They'll always have jobs, they'll always be in demand, and they'll always have employment. They might get paid over scale. They may be tapped to move up to foreman or superintendent. They might get a truck. Contractors will often keep the elite on the payroll even when there's no work, just to keep from losing them to another company. These might be tomorrow's contractors. This is their reward for being top performers, for having the best skills, attitudes, and behaviors.

The Good Guys: Middle Performers (30-50 percent)

The middle 30-50 percent are the "good guys" on the job. On time, fine attitude, and good skills—that's what the good guys are all about. They have what it takes to be good journeymen. They're valued by their employers. They're dependable. They're not always pushing their limits or building new skills, but they can be relied on to move the job forward.

The Fill-In Guys: Marginal Performers (20-30 percent)

The fill-in guys make up another 20-30 percent. Fill-in guys get most of their hours when it's busy, and they usually don't stay with a contractor very long. This group is weak in some basic area of skills, attitude, or behavior, and it shows. They're never "lead-men" on the job. They'll get fewer hours overall unless the market is totally booming. They're close to the last guys hired and usually the first to be laid off. This group ranges from average to below average in their skills, behaviors, and attitudes.

The Bottom: Poor Performers (5-10 percent)

The bottom 5-10 percent are a problem. They generally lack the skills, attitudes, and/or behaviors to be successful in our business. Most of the time they don't even know it (or don't want to know). They hurt the image of union construction every day. They're the ones employers are thinking about when they're wondering why in the hell they should have to pay higher union wages for such lame-ass workers. They're keeping us all from "growing the pie." They go from employer-to-employer and job site-to-job site because they either have bad attitudes or they just can't get it done. Maybe the real problem is that they just don't care enough.

Ask yourself this: Which category am I in *today*? Ask yourself which category you want to be in. Ask yourself what you need to do to move up?

The Guy Next to You Needs to be a Winner

When you look at these differences in your fellow workers, you need to think about how it impacts you. Does it piss you off sometimes that you're making the same hourly rate as the guy next to you who couldn't even tie your shoes? Well, guess what? You've got a much bigger problem than that right now. That guy may have a lot to do with how much you make years and years from now.

Union contractors pay a certain amount per hour, which is determined through the bargaining process with the union. Most of the time, all the guys on the job will get paid pretty much the same. Think about it for a second—are contractors going to want to pay more than what the worst guy on the job is worth?

Looking at it from the other direction, do you think they'd be willing to pay more if everybody had stronger skills, higher productivity, and better attitudes? I'm guessing they probably would. So when you look at the guy on the job next to you who's not pulling his weight, you've got to ask yourself this: "Is he helping to increase my next raise, or is he holding it back?" There's no in-between.

Winning Through **Productivity**

Winning this fight is about two things: quality and production. How much the team gets done, and how fast and how good is it when it is done. So how much "hands-on work" gets done by a regular construction team during a regular day? Eight hours? Not even close. According to an industry study, only about one third of the average workday is spent on "direct work." Here's how the study* breaks down how the average construction worker's time is spent on most job sites:

Activity	Percentage of workday
Direct work being performed	32%
Waiting time / delays	29%
Travel time	13%
Receiving instructions	8%
Tools, material, and set-up	7%
Late starts and early quits	6%
Personal breaks	5%
Total for workday	100%

(* Source: 2001 AACE International)

Why does this matter? It matters because productivity is all we've got; it's how we're going to beat non-union labor. Unless we want to compete by reducing wages and fringes, competing on productivity is the only way we can do it. Of course, in different kinds of work and projects, these productivity percentages change a lot. But there are little things we can do on every job to make sure we score higher on productivity every single day.

Here are ten quick tips for boosting your productivity numbers:

1. Use waiting time to plan ahead for work to come.
2. Don't start late.
3. Don't quit early.
4. When traveling, go directly to and from jobs.
5. Check to see that you have all the materials and tools you need before you leave, then check again.
6. Don't extend personal breaks or tolerate others that do.
7. Give instructions to apprentices or others needing direction before they need it, not while they are doing it.
8. When it's practical, take your bathroom and smoking breaks during waiting times.
9. Stay focused on task completion and quality.
10. Set goals for work you want to complete by a certain time. You get more done and the day goes faster.

A Winning Investment in You

Making and molding an elite warrior is not cheap. It takes a bucket of cash to train an apprentice through journeyman. After you weed out all the dropouts and duds (10+ percent in most crafts), it's not unusual for unions and contractors to spend from $10,000 to $30,000 to graduate an apprentice. Yeah, I know—it costs that much to go to college! And you don't even get to go to keggers!

Still, it's a great education, no matter how you look at it. Every year, unions and employers spend hundreds of millions of dollars to train the workforce. That's a hefty price tag for making you the best in the world. In return, you're only asked to do one thing. And if you haven't figured out what it is by now, do us all a favor—toss this book and go get a job driving a bus.

(And the answer is: *To be one of the best union construction journeymen in the world*)

Your Career is Your Business

Your job isn't guaranteed. You live from job-to-job in this business, from dispatch-to-dispatch. You are directly responsible for your value on the job. Your ability to thrive and make money is directly related to the skills, attitudes, and behaviors you bring to the job. These things determine how many hours you work each week, month, and year. They'll be reflected in how long you stay with a contractor, and they'll determine how much he values your contribution. Your job is your business. Manage it well.

The Winner's Reward: Finding a Home

There is such a thing as finding a "home" in the construction business. Your home is a company where you'll work for years. A company that knows you can deliver results and appreciates it. Your job is to find this place and then work to belong there. This is how you combine your job and your life in a way that makes both a whole lot better.

A good company will know you when they see you. Not all of them, of course; some contractors are too big, too small, or just too dumb to understand. But some of them want to find you just as bad as you want to find them. And once they do find you, they'll show their appreciation by keeping you on. For months or years—or even decades. There are plenty of guys who find their home and never take another dispatch. Why? Because they showed the contractor from day one that they were different.

Smart contractors have a good eye for talent, and they're constantly on the lookout for it. They don't even care if they need anybody right now; if they find somebody good, they'll find a place for them. They know that if they let a great worker go, he'll get snapped up by another company in a heartbeat, and they don't want to see that happen.

Nobody's going to give you a home on a silver platter; you have to earn it. Not everybody is in an area or industry where it's even possible, but if you can make it happen, it'll bring you far greater earnings and stability over your career than you'll have otherwise. Trust me, it's something worth aiming for.

Chapter Four

Tradition and Reputation

"Whatever you are, be a good one."

—Abraham Lincoln

Company Performance Profile:
Harley Davidson, Inc.

Title of Profile: **Reputation Sells**

Profile: Harley Davidson Motorcycles

Key to Success: Recreating an image of quality, attitude, and American pride

Backed It Up: Went from making leaky, defect-ridden bikes as a subsidiary of a sporting goods company (AMF Corporation, which made bowling balls) to regaining its independence, making quality its number-one priority and becoming one of the most well-recognized, well-respected brand names in the world.

Lesson: American pride and American-made are not enough. They have to prove themselves in action.

Tradition: a Foundation for the Future

Tradition can be the foundation for a great future. It's why we have so many grandfathers, fathers, sons, and daughters in this business, generation after generation. Tradition is a powerful thing, but it has a downside, too, namely, hanging on to beliefs, actions, or behaviors that no longer work.

In the 1960s and 70s, unions had some beliefs and traditions that were hard-core. Even when contractors turned their backs, they still didn't change. And even when major plants and manufacturers kicked out union contractors and workers because of the old traditions, things still didn't change. It took years of getting our asses kicked in the marketplace to understand that maybe the old ways weren't the best ways after all.

Never turn your back on tradition; it's made plenty of unions and contractors great organizations. On the other hand, never lean on traditions that have outlived their usefulness. You'll know the difference.

Street Credentials:
Union Reputations Today

How does the marketplace see union workers today? You know, all those people who don't know yet that you're the best in the world. What negative stereotypes and images are out there? What kinds of messages about unions and union workers are being put out by the media?

Let's face it, sometimes it's not pretty, and often times the things people believe aren't true. But if they believe them, they might as well be true. For example, take a look at the following statements:

- "Union workers are overpaid."
- "Union workers are hard to deal with."
- "Union workers take things for granted."
- "Union workers are spoiled."
- "Union workers are no better than non-union workers."
- "Union workers are inefficient."
- "Unions protect bad apples."
- "Union workers have bad attitudes."

Are any of these statements true? Look around your job site. What do you see? Does it even matter? When you think about it, the real problem we face is not whether the negative images are true; it's whether the marketplace *believes* they're true. It's not 1960 anymore, but some people still see unions that way because that's the way they've been shown in movies and on TV. Unions and union workers are different now—a lot different. A lot more consistent and cooperative. And a lot more competitive.

What would it take to get people to believe the exact opposite of each of the statements above?

- ■ "Union workers are worth every penny."
- ■ "Union workers are a pleasure to deal with."
- ■ "Union workers take nothing for granted."
- ■ "Union workers have a 'can-do' attitude."
- ■ "Union workers work their butts off for everything they've got."
- ■ "Union workers are light years ahead of non-union workers."
- ■ "Union workers are unbelievably efficient."
- ■ "Unions don't tolerate slackers."
- ■ "Union workers have outstanding attitudes."
- ■ "Union workers are always a better value."

What would it take? Just this: Make sure we're the best in the whole damn world and then tell the whole damn world about it.

Old School Says, New School Says

Old school says:
- We never did it that way…
- We don't have to change…
- We don't like new ideas and approaches, but we don't have any ideas of our own.

New school says:
- Let's build on how we used to do it…
- If we don't change, we can't get better…
- Let's take risks if it means a better deal for all of us in the long run.

Construction Unions:
Not All are Created Equal

In the old days, union solidarity was the only way to go. *Stand up for all your union brothers, right or wrong. Stand tall with the labor movement.* It was all part of pride and tradition, and it's how the labor movement became powerful.

Today it's hard to ignore the differences among construction unions. The truth is, some crafts are moving forward, but others are still stuck in the past. In ten years, some crafts will be thriving, while others will be struggling, or maybe gone. Some crafts will work toward a better deal for everybody; others will look for a better deal for themselves. And some won't do jack shit; they'll be the ball and chain the rest of us have to drag around.

Three **Types** of Unions:
A Building Trades Check-Up

In your local union building trades, there are likely three types of unions; they look and sound something like this:

Smart unions moving forward: Smart unions deal honestly with their members, take the right risks (sometimes pissing off the old-school members in the process), and get results. They have decent relationships with their contractors, and they're busy organizing new contractors and getting more projects. They're not looking at their own internal politics as the most important thing. They are doing a great job at training and retraining. They're aggressively organizing and growing the pie for their members and contractors. These unions are the leaders, and it's their members who'll benefit the most.

Unions that are facing change and are not too happy about it: These unions are just starting to change. Maybe some of the membership isn't too happy about it, so they're dragging their feet. Maybe they have really bad relations with their contractors, so everything is always about conflict. Maybe the business manager is a new guy trying to get on his feet. These guys will probably make it, but it's going to take a while.

Unions in denial: These unions have leadership that isn't doing anything. Maybe they're just trying to protect the status quo at election time. Maybe somebody doesn't want to take any risks or do anything different, no matter how important it is. Or maybe the business manager is a great guy and leader, but there's a small (and loud) group of rank-and-file guys who won't let change happen. It could be that this very vocal group makes it close to impossible for the union to move forward. Without change, this union's future is one of fewer members, hours, and opportunities.

Bottom line: Unions are like businesses. Each one is going to take a different approach. The ones that are moving forward aggressively, like any good business, are going to do well, and so will their members. The ones sitting on their asses are going down sooner or later. Here are some of the hard questions that lie ahead:

- Should every construction union support every other union, all the time, right or wrong?
- If another union isn't getting the job done, or if it's standing in your way, what should happen?

I'm not saying I have the answers, but these are things we all need to think about, and the sooner the better.

Union Pride = Self Pride

If you spend any time on the highway, you'll see a lot of bumper stickers that say things like, "Union Pride," or "Proud to Be Union." What does it really mean? Union pride is about *self*-pride. It's about standing up for and with your union, through your performance and commitment.

What union pride is not about is standing *behind* your union, expecting it to make excuses for why you can't get the job done. Union pride is not one of your guaranteed benefits you get by making your monthly dues payments. Union pride is *earned*.

Union pride is earned every time you go the extra mile to get the job done right. It's earned by encouraging others to do the same. It's earned by keeping up your skills and learning new ones. It's earned by getting out of the mindset of, "what am I getting in return for paying my dues every month?" and into the idea of, "how am I supporting a positive union image every single day on the job?" It's not what you put on your bumper; it's what you do on and off the job every day.

The "Union Yes" Promise:

Quality, Excellence, and Value

"Price is what you pay. Value is what you get."

—Warren Buffet

45

Performance Profile: Wayne Gretzky

Title of Profile: **The Great One**

Name: Wayne Gretzky

Profile: Twenty seasons as the greatest hockey player in the history of the world.

Key to Success: Used natural skills, competitive fire, and team orientation to win everywhere he went, with every team he played on. Plus, everyone liked and respected him wherever he went.

Backed it Up: NHL all time points, assists, and goals. Four Stanley Cups. Nine years MVP. Fifteen-time All Star. Holds 61 NHL Records.

Lesson: Skills, attitude, and behaviors all contribute to his value as the greatest to play his game.

Value: We Cost More (And Better be Worth It)

When you go to buy something, how do you decide which brand you want? Is it only about price? Whatever is the easiest to find? Other reasons? Consider these choices:

Hyundai vs. GM or Ford

Craftsman vs. Buffalo Tools

Red Wing vs. Payless Shoes

Made in USA vs. Made in China

People buy things based on *value*. They ask themselves, *what am I getting for my money?* You do it. We all do. We're all willing to pay more if we think we're getting a better overall value. Union construction is always more expensive than non-union because it's a better value. We're never going to compete on price; they can always go cheaper than us. We compete by making sure *the quality and speed of our work makes it a better value.*

Union Yes Value vs. the Wal-Mart World

We now live in a Wal-Mart world. Wal-Mart is the biggest retailer in the world mostly because most people don't care as much about others as they do about getting the best deal for themselves. Pretty sad and selfish in some ways, but that's what we have to deal with. A lot of people will cry and complain, but that won't put one more guy to work.

In the Wal-Mart world, everyone wants to know one thing: *What have you done for me today at the best possible price?* That is the question that everyone is asking union contractors and workers. They say, hey we are paying more to use you than to use non-union, so, *what have you done for me today at that price?* It is not enough to say, well, we took good care of families. We set people up for a stable retirement. We helped the community. The Wal-Mart world and today's marketplace will give us two words in return: *F--k that.* Cruel, brutal, and unforgiving.

The market does not care. It only wants to hear about value, return on investment, and the bottom line. So the Wal-Mart world and the competitive marketplace will stick its ugly mug right in our face and ask again, "Now, like I asked you before, *what have you done for me today at the best possible price?"*

And our answer must be: We gave you more than you paid for, more than you asked for, and more than you expected. (Asshole!)

Union Yes: Our Bumper Sticker Promise

What are we going to tell the market about the fact that we are the best value in the world? How about the worn-out slogan, "Union Yes"?

☐ "Union Yes" is on 100,000 truck bumpers.

☐ "Union Yes" is a nice little feel-good, meaningless slogan.

☐ "Union Yes" doesn't tell me what value is in it for me when I use union construction.

■ "Union Yes" is an incomplete sentence.

When we approach contractors and project owners, developers, and others, we've got to make the *Union Yes* slogan into the *Union Yes* promise:

■ "UNION: YES, we are more *productive.*"

☐ "UNION: YES, we are a better *value.*"

☐ "UNION: YES, we are higher *quality.*"

■ "UNION: YES, we have great *attitudes.*"

■ "UNION: YES, we are *safer.*"

☐ "UNION: YES, we are *worth the extra money.*"

☐ "UNION: YES, we are *the best in the world.*"

These are the real messages that we need to get out there.

The Real Cost of Union "Value"

Value is about getting what you pay for. So let's look at what the contractor pays for when he hires a union guy on his payroll. Strange but true—what you get paid is not the same as how much you cost the contractor. When a union contractor hires you, he has to pay social security, payroll tax, workers compensation, disability insurance, and more—on every hour you get paid for. In construction, it usually adds 40 percent to the contractor's cost, even though you never see it. Forty percent more! All this goes into his bids when competing with non-union contractors.

So for example, if you're getting a $35 an hour total package, that means it costs the contractor around $50 per hour. Why is this important? Because that's the cost the contractor has to use to bid the job to get the work. You might be getting paid $300 a shift, but it's costing the contractor $500. And that's the cost he has to pass on to the project owner. That's the cost he's using to compete against non-union contractors.

It's important to know that the contractor is planning on getting a certain amount of work done for every dollar he pays out, including the ones you never see. Value has a big dollar cost to the contractor (and his client) and it's important to remember that fact.

The Team Cost of Union "Value"

Now that we've looked at what the contractor pays you, let's look at a job site team. How much does a crew cost per hour, day, week, month, and year? Who cares? We all should. Here's why:

The contractor always bids jobs based on his best estimate of crew cost and production. If he figures right he makes money. If he figures wrong he loses money, and maybe his whole company. The thing is, his profit can disappear fast if crew costs don't match his estimated production.

For example, let's say a contractor is bidding on a job. Here's how he might figure his crew costs, based on eight journeymen:

Eight journeymen at a total wage-and-fringe package of $40 per hour each. Add all the costs the government makes the contractor pay (that you never see), including unemployment insurance and workers compensation, and it adds up to about 40 percent on top of the $40. So that means each worker costs around $60 per hour.

8 journeymen x $60 cost per hour	= $480 every hour
$480 cost per hour x 8 hours	= $3,840 every day
$3,840 per day x 5 days per week	= $19,200 every week
$19,200 per week x 4.3 weeks per month	= $82,560 every month

It adds up to some big numbers quick, doesn't it? Now maybe you can understand why the contractor gets a little touchy when his estimates of production don't match up to those heavy dollars.

Now let's look at some common delays that can slow down the job and how much they might cost using the numbers above:

Waiting for materials to be delivered:
40 minutes (2/3 hour) x $480   = $320 loss

One guy doesn't show up and
delays a pour or installation:
2 hours x $480   = $960 loss

Problems with another
sub-contractor in the way:
6 hours x $480   = $2,880 loss

It doesn't take a math wiz to see that these numbers can add up fast. None of these things were planned by the contractor. For him to get the job, he figured that every dollar spent for labor meant something getting done.

So when the contractor looks at crew costs, he's not planning on John or Mike or Jose leaving something at the yard and spending 45 minutes going back to fetch it. He's not thinking that the foreman might forget a critical step in prep work one day and lose two hours. He's not planning on the concrete, wire, steel, asphalt, jacks, welding gear, fuel truck, pump truck, drywall, or anything else not being there when they're needed. He's not planning on the concrete truck being late or the other subcontractor being in the way. When it does happen, it's his ass and money on the line. Lots of small hits are just as bad as one really big hit, and they can drive a union contractor out of business. And that means we all lose.

What am I getting at? Value is about getting the best deal from money spent. Value added or taken away is driven by cost. Workers standing around cost as much as workers doing productive work. That's the simple version of crew costs. It adds up quick whether you're making it or losing it.

What If It Was You: Value and Quality

When you go to buy a product, do you just look for whatever's cheapest? Do you buy the cheapest tools, cars, guns, boats, beer, diapers, and condoms? I'm guessing not. I'm guessing you shop for quality and value. So when you spend *your* cold, hard cash, you have some expectations. Let me ask you:

- What if you bought a new Harley and it had an oil leak?
- What if you bought a new Maytag washer and it shredded your clothes?
- What if you bought a new Dell laptop and it wouldn't boot up?
- What if you bought a new Calloway driver and it had a loose head?
- What if you bought a new Remington and it misfired?
- What if you bought a new DeWalt cordless drill and the battery pack wouldn't charge?
- What if you bought a new F-150 and the engine light came on?

Would you be happy? Not even—you'd be pissed off! Would you think about making a different choice next time?

It's the same with union construction. Every day, we ask developers and companies to use union contractors and workers even though we're more expensive. We have to provide more value. If they pay a premium and then don't get premium work and productivity, they're going to feel cheated and dissatisfied. Plus, next time, they're a lot more likely to go non-union.

When you pay more, you expect more. If you get it, you'll buy again next time. It's the same for the people who hire you.

Performance Profile: Tiger Woods

Title of Profile: **Practicing Excellence**

Name: Tiger Woods

Profile: Young player became the best in the world with a single-minded focus on excellence and perfection. Practices four-to-six hours every day. Uses two coaches at all times. Absolutely focused on being the best and will accept no less from himself.

Key to Success: Never eased up on himself, even after he became #1 golfer in the world. Total competitive fire. Compares himself to his own best effort.

Backed it Up: Won the PGA Grand Slam, four Masters Tournaments, two U.S. Opens, and two PGA Championships. Career winnings: $39,700,000. Endorsement money: they don't make numbers big enough to count it.

Lesson: Excellence does not come naturally. You have to focus on it and practice at it. You are never good enough, especially when everyone else thinks so.

Excellence: Zero Re-work Required

**"If you don't have time to do it right
the first time, when are you going to have time
to re-do it?"**

—old construction saying

Shabby, poor quality work that has to be done over does not reflect excellence. Re-work means someone is not committed to excellence. Re-work kills the value of union construction. Reasons for re-work usually include one or more of the following:

- Work done in a hurry without eye to detail
- Wrong tools or materials
- No consideration for quality; didn't care
- Unfinished business
- Poor supervision
- Material defect
- Poor final inspection or testing
- Corners cut
- Skill level not sufficient for work

Trouble is, re-work is at least twice as expensive as doing it right the first time. Don't be the reason the cost on your job doubles. Most of the problems listed above can be dealt with on the front end. Pay attention to the details *before* they become expensive re-work problems.

One Small Mistake

How does rework happen? How do whole projects get messed up? Easy. One small mistake at a time. Any one little mistake might seem insignificant at the time, but even minor mistakes can turn into major problems later on—after it's too late.

> The right offensive guard
> For the top team in the NFL
> Isn't paying attention
> On just one play
> And missed his block
> A small mistake
> One out of 200 plays
> And the linebacker got by him
> And blindsided the quarterback
> Who lost the fumble
> In the fourth quarter
> With nine seconds to go
> On third and goal
> At the one yard line
> In the Super Bowl.

Hey, what's one little mistake?

Chapter Six

Personal Responsibility

"It is not up to anyone else to
make me give my best."

—Hakeem Olajumon, NBA

Performance Profile: Pat Tillman

Title of Profile: **Do the Right Thing for Yourself**

Name: Pat Tillman

Profile: Arizona Cardinals linebacker with $3 million contract. Walked away from football and volunteered for military service after the 9-11 terrorist attacks. Refused to give interviews and discouraged special attention from the press. Became an elite Army Ranger fighting in Afghanistan. Killed in action. Awarded the Silver Star and the Purple Heart.

Key to Success: Followed his own convictions no matter what. Did not take the easy way even though no one would have blamed him if he had. Was willing to risk everything for his convictions, beliefs, and personal honor.

Backed It Up: Walked away from a sure thing—fame and fortune as a pro ball player—for his own beliefs.

Lesson: Do what you think is right no matter what anyone else does or tells you. Be your own person even if it's the hard choice.

Your Own Responsibilities

Being the best in the world on the job comes with some basic responsibilities. They aren't complicated, but they are necessary. They include:

- Being on time every day
- Showing up for work every day unless you're really sick
- Putting in eight hours work for eight hours pay
- Being clean and sober at work
- Being highly productive all day
- Having a good attitude with your team, the contractor, and the project owner
- Thinking about costs and doing your part to control them
- Taking pride in quality workmanship
- Showing respect and tolerance for everyone on the job site
- Following directions from foremen and supervisors
- Being ethical and honest at all times
- Practicing safe, smart work habits
- Being willing to learn
- Being willing to teach
- Being loyal to your union
- Being loyal to your employer
- Leading by example
- Being open to changes and improvement
- Understanding and supporting teamwork

Pump Up Your ABS: Attitude Before Skill

Ask any foreman, superintendent, or contractor: *Would you rather have a guy with awesome skills and a poor attitude, or a guy with poor skills and an awesome attitude?* They'll go with attitude every time. Wouldn't you? It's always attitude before skill. And nothing's more important as a building block for your own success.

Honesty and Integrity

Seems like every day there's some business, political, or religious leader in the news for lying, cheating, or stealing. What leads to a breakdown in basic honesty and integrity in an organization? No one seeing or believing in the value of being honest. No one being willing to take a stand on values. No one being willing to put aside self-interest and greed to do the right thing.

It only takes one person to set that example. In government, a company, a union, or even on a job site. Be that person. Be that example. Do the right thing because you want to, not because you have to.

What If It Was You: Honesty and Integrity

Let's say you're at the pool. Your kid is playing with a squishy toy you bought for $4. Some other kid picks it up and walks off. Are you going to let him keep it? Of course not. You're going to get it back. It is your kid's squishy toy, and you'll be damned if you're going to let some other kid steal it, even though it is just four bucks. It's just plain wrong, right?

What about taking off with materials or tools from the job site? Is that OK? It's just some 2x4s...a wrench...saw...nail gun...compressor...Some guys treat the job site like it's their own personal Home Depot. You know who I'm talking about.

Call it whatever you want, but it's stealing and it's wrong. Doesn't matter whether it's a four-dollar squishy or an eight hundred-dollar compressor. You wouldn't look the other way if somebody stole your kid's squishy. You shouldn't tolerate rip-offs on the job site either.

Setting the Pace

Who sets the pace on your job? Besides the foreman, the top guys on the crew usually set the pace. Within one hour on any job site, you'll know if the guys are working up to their potential. Here's a piece of advice: set your own pace, and make it challenging and interesting for yourself. You might take a little heat if you're pushing, but remember, time flies when you're flying and it drags when you're dragging.

Side Job-Itis

There's a condition that can seriously impact you if you're not careful. It's called side job-itis. It's highly contagious, especially when work is slow. Or when you're on the bottom of the list. Or when your kid needs braces.

Side job-itis can hurt your fellow union members and union contractors. You should avoid it whenever possible. But if you do catch a case of it, don't ever use your contractor's tools, equipment, or materials anywhere except on his job site. If you do, bad things can happen. Spread the word. You heard it from Dr. Breslin.

Job Site Negativity and Gossip

You're going to be spending 20 years on the job site. You'll work with a lot of guys. You'll talk about a lot of things during breaks, lunch, and so on. So what? So this: some people spend all their time talking about other people on the job. Others just want to complain about the boss, their job, the weather, whatever. You name it, they'll think of something negative to say.

Don't be that guy. You can decide what's worth talking about. Why does it matter? Because you're part of a team out there on the job site every day. I'm not saying everybody has to like everybody else, but if someone is just complaining full-time it can get out of control.

Negativity always feeds negativity. Take responsibility for being a positive job site force. Make sure you're not dragging a black cloud behind you. If you are, I have a secret I want to share with you. Nobody really gives a shit, and most of them aren't even listening anyway.

Our Community Image 24/7

Did your mom and dad want you to be a union craft worker? I hope so. I hope you're lucky enough to be a third or fourth-generation construction guy like I am. But most of you aren't. And most moms and dads these days want their kids to go to college for a different kind of job. Maybe you do, too.

A lot of it has to do with the image of the construction industry. Some people still have the wrong image of construction workers. The old image of a bunch of dirty, rude, unskilled guys yelling at girls is still going strong. The myth that construction is for people who can't do anything better is out there, too.

It's time to change those old ideas, and that is part of our personal responsibility. Here are some things to think about, talk about, and remember:

- The average union construction worker makes more than the average computer worker.
- The average union construction worker has to have strong technical ability to do his job well.
- The average union construction guy has better benefits than the average big company employee.
- There are more than 2 million union construction workers. Hundreds of training schools teach them every day of every year.
- Construction employs more people in North America than most any other industry.
- Construction workers use high-technology equipment

like lasers and computer programs.

- Construction makes people's lives easier and better.
- Construction is a profession.

It's up to us to show people that construction is a profession worthy of respect. There are plenty of great kids who would be awesome in our industry. Why aren't they interested in construction? Part of it is that we carry an old image that's dead and should've been buried a long time ago. Do your part to bury it for good. Be a respectable, responsible professional in every way.

Wearing YOUR colors

It's important to keep in mind that you represent your union on and off the job site. Are you flipping people off in traffic with your "Union Pride" sticker in the window? Are you wearing your union shirt or jacket to the ballgame and getting drunk or being a wild man?

On the other hand, do you let people know that you're a union construction worker when you're volunteering, coaching, or working at your church?

Just like every Marine in uniform represents the entire Marine Corps, every union construction worker represents all 2 million of the team. Wear your colors with pride and class. And if you have to act like an idiot, do everyone a favor: don't advertise that you're a union-affiliated knucklehead.

Work Ethic,
Commitment,
and
Attitude

"Motivation is simple. You eliminate those who
are not motivated."

—Lou Holtz, Notre Dame Coach

Performance Profile: Aaron Ralston

Title of Profile: **Committed to the Bone**

Name: Aaron Ralston

Profile: Rock climber spent five days alone in a remote canyon with his hand and arm pinned under a two-ton boulder. Facing certain death, he broke his own arm, then cut off his own hand and forearm with a Leatherman to save his life.

Key to Success: Recognize what you have to do and then do it, no matter what.

Backed it Up: After five days with no food and little water, Ralston cut off his arm, climbed up a 100-foot canyon, roped down a 75-foot cliff, then hiked seven miles in 95-degree desert heat before being rescued.

Lesson: Face reality. Take responsibility for yourself through your commitment.

Entitled to What?

Maybe you think being a union guy entitles you to special privileges. That certain perks come with the territory. Well, I've got news for you: nobody's entitled to anything.

In union construction, there are no guarantees or special considerations. For anybody. It doesn't matter if your grandfather or your dad was in the union. It doesn't matter if you "know" people. When you join, you get exactly one thing: an opportunity to prove that you've got what it takes to be one of the best in the world.

This chapter is about how to make that opportunity work for you.

Making a Contribution (Big or Small)

A good hand is always looking for ways to contribute. Doing something—anything—is always better than standing around doing nothing. Worried about getting yelled at for doing something you shouldn't be? Well, you'll definitely get yelled at if you stand around with your thumb up your...well, you get the idea.

Once, when I was a rookie, I dragged a bunch of screw jacks through mud up to my knees on a freezing morning. Nobody asked me to do it. I just saw that it needed to get done, and I did it. That was the day I made the team. Nobody said anything, but the journeymen treated me differently after that. It doesn't have to be a big deal. Clean something. Move something. Lay something out for the next section of work. Think ahead. Plan ahead. Work ahead. Look around for something to do.

What If It Was You: Giving Your Best Effort

Imagine your kid needed life-or-death surgery. What if the surgeon showed up late for the operation, talked the whole time, didn't use his instruments right, took a bunch of breaks, and wanted to leave early? You'd wish you hired a different surgeon (besides wanting to kick his ass). Well, no matter if you're a doctor, lawyer, craftsman, or cop, you've got to be committed. Your level of commitment on the job site every day will make the difference whether union construction lives or dies.

Individual Performance Profile:
Cal Ripkin, Jr.

Title of Profile: **The Iron Man**

Profile: Baseball player going into the Hall of Fame on the first ballot. Not the best player at his position, but he played in more games without missing one than anyone else. Went to work sick, hurt, tired, and discouraged. Inspired everyone around him with his work ethic and will of iron.

Key to Success: Go in every day to contribute, no matter what.

Backed It Up: 2131 games in a row.

Lesson: There is no substitute for an awesome work ethic. It reveals the individual and inspires everyone around them.

Being There Matters

Being at work every day matters. It matters a lot. Some guys think, *what's the difference if I show up or not?* What is the difference? What if you were a NASCAR driver and one of your pit crew didn't show up for an important race? Now your crew boss will have to reassign somebody. Of course, that guy won't be quite as good at his job as the guy who didn't show. You'll lose seconds on your pit stops, and in tough competition you need every edge.

When you run short, you can't win. There's confusion and delay. And if the missing guy has a key job, the entire team can fall apart. Every guy on every job is important. Without you, there's a hole that has to be filled. Without you, the team isn't as effective and competitive as it needs to be. Even if you feel burnt, bummed, or raw in the morning, just drag your butt out of bed and go. They need you.

The Dumbest Thing I Ever Heard

A young guy on a job site told me once, "Hey, the boss should be happy I didn't come in. Now he doesn't have to pay me." Hey, genius, what do you think it cost that boss to:

- Run the crew shorthanded?
- Take a guy off another job?
- Delay or cancel that part of the job?
- Have too few guys doing too much work (safety impact)?
- Have another union do that work instead of him?
- Call the hall and get somebody raw and late to replace him?

Yeah, the boss just can't believe his good luck.

The Long Weekend

Absenteeism is a huge problem, especially before and after weekends. Almost 75 percent of no-shows happen on Fridays and Mondays. Doing a little hunting, fishing, or skiing? Need an extra day and figure you can just give the boss a B.S. story? Just don't run out of dead aunts and grandparents…

So you don't feel like going in. What do you think it's going to be like for the guys who have to cover for you? How do you think that feels? Trust me, it gets old real fast.

Everybody has to have a life. Nobody wants to grind it out every single day. But leaving your crew short so you can have your own personal holiday is just a lie in action. If this is you, don't do it. If you don't do it, don't tolerate it on your crew either.

No-Shows Cost You a 60" Plasma TV, a trip to Hawaii, and a Few Cold Ones

If you are absent (by your own choice) six extra days a year for long weekends or whatever, what does it cost you over a year? Over your career?

- *Six days each year*

  6 days = 48 hours x $35 total package = $1680 out of your pocket

- *Six days each year for your career*

  6 days x 25 years = 1200 hours x $35 total package = $42,000 out of your pocket

By the way, $42,000 will buy you a 60" plasma screen TV, 10 years of cable, a family trip to Hawaii (for about two months), a custom-engraved shotgun, and a six-pack of cold ones.

Transportation is a Lame Ass Excuse

This is going to be short and sweet. Make sure that you have dependable transportation. Make sure your car or truck starts every time. Take care of it so it'll take care of you. "My truck won't start" is an excuse that doesn't fly more than once. And if you get your license yanked, make sure you have buddies lined up who're willing to take your gas money.

What If It Was You: Transportation

Let's say you've got fifty-yard-line tickets to the NFL Playoffs. You and your buddy have been hoping all season to see this game. A half hour before the tailgate party, your buddy calls and tells you his car won't start. You're going to miss the first quarter at least. What are you going to tell him? That you understand and it's no problem? No way. You're going to be pissed off, and that's putting it mildly. Are you going to blame him or his car?

Just Give Me a Break

How many breaks do you take in a day? How many do you need? Some guys take a pee break, then a smoke break, then a coffee break. Then they get a long break while waiting for materials. You get the picture. On some jobs there's a lot of waiting time. On others there isn't any. Stuff happens. You've got to be flexible.

You don't want to be abused, but neither does the contractor. Breaks add up, and they cut into workflow and productivity. You want to spend your day drinking coffee and taking tons of breaks? Here's a career tip: go to work for the government.

What If It Was You: Late Starts

Let's say you hired Tom the handyman to paint your back porch and replace your garbage disposal. You're going to pay Tom $20 an hour. On the first day, you see Tom out in his truck at 8:00 a.m. drinking coffee. After he finishes his coffee he gets his tools together, comes in, lays out his stuff, and gets to work around eight fifteen.

No big deal, right? But let's say you notice Tom doing this every day. And at the end of the week when he hands you his bill, and he's charging from 8:00 each day. What are you going to do? Are you going to pay him the 1 ¼ hours for his morning coffee drinking? He thinks it was part of his work day. Do you?

You wouldn't pay somebody for drinking coffee and *getting ready* to work. You pay them to work. Why should anybody pay you unless you're working? On a union job site, the work begins when the shift begins.

If you're wondering what's the big deal with a few minutes a day, think about this: a late start, ten minutes a day, adds up to 215 minutes (over three hours) per month or 2580 minutes (43 hours!) a year. That's more than one whole week—of being paid for doing nothing. At $50 total cost, that's $2,000 per year. Who can afford that in a competitive marketplace? And that's only ten minutes. On plenty of job sites, late starts can go fifteen minutes or more.

You'd never put up with this if it was your money. Be just as tough-minded when you're on the job site. Be ready to work when the shift begins.

What If It Was You: Leaving Early

Let's say you went to the barbershop for your monthly trim. Your barber cuts your hair on one side, and then he just stops and asks for his money. Says he needs to cut out a few minutes early today. What are you going to do? Give him his money and enjoy your new look? No way. You're going to tell him he'd better finish the job right now. And next time you're going to switch to Supercuts.

So why do some guys in the union construction business leave before the shift is over? Maybe they think they're entitled to it. Maybe that was the old way of doing business. But what if you were paying the tab?

Job Walk Offs and Disruptions

Walking off or disrupting a job is one of the worst things you can do as a union craftsperson. Don't do it. Some guys think that jurisdiction is worth a walk-off. Some guys think their own personal beef is worth a slow-down or disruption. Some guys think that what other crafts are doing or not doing is worth a walk-off. Some guys are missing the boat.

The only acceptable reason for walking off the job is a major safety issue—and I'm not talking some petty stuff, either. I'm talking about risking life and limb. If that's the case, and the foreman refuses to do anything about it, *then* you can walk. Just be sure to report the incident to your union immediately.

No working person in America or Canada walks off the job. From a janitor at McDonalds to the President of the United States. From cops and firemen, to nurses and soldiers. Nobody else does it, and we're no different. Even if you think you're getting the short end of the stick somehow, you can't just walk. Walk-offs are one of the reasons we lost our asses in the marketplace. Project owners will go non-union every time if we pull this stuff.

Jurisdiction: Not a License to Lounge

Some guys don't want to do anything outside their work or craft. "It's not *my* job." Fine. But if you think you're helping the union movement by standing around while another union guy busts his ass, you are sadly mistaken. Everybody on the job needs to play their "A" game as a team.

You're not too important to do whatever is needed. Nobody is. In the NFL, even the quarterback has to block on a reverse, even if he gets flattened. It's a matter of pride to contribute. Don't abuse jurisdiction, but don't use it as an excuse either.

Stay Off The Cell

Let's keep this simple. The only people who talk on the phone at work are directory assistance, telephone solicitors and "hot talk" porn operators. Unless you are one of these, (and I am sincerely hoping you are not) stay off your phone at work. No one else answers a cell phone, interrupts their work and talks while others are working unless it is a family emergency. Your date for Friday is not a family emergency. Stay off the phone at work.

Care of Tools

A lot of guys look at the contractor's tools as disposable items. Goggles, gloves, shovels, wrenches, pumps, jacks, and other small tools. They act like tools and equipment grow on trees and it doesn't matter if they lose or break them. What about you? Do you think it matters?

What If It Was You: Your Tools

Let's say your neighbor comes over to borrow your drill. He still hasn't returned the level and the WD-40 he borrowed a few weeks ago. You bring it up. He says, "Well, you can just buy some other ones right?"

What are you going to do, hand over your DeWalt? Yeah, right! You're going to tell him you want your stuff back, and no, he can't borrow your drill. It's the same way on the job. Treat your employers' tools like they were your own.

The Crew: Brothers, Bastards, or Both?

Who is "the crew" on a job site? A lot of changing faces, all working toward a common goal. At its best, it makes you happy to go to work each day. At its worst, it'll make you want to spend a lot more time with your old pal Bud Weiser.

At its best, the crew is:

■ A bunch of rowdy brothers

■ A NASCAR pit crew

■ An NFL Pro Bowl starting team

■ A well oiled machine

■ A great group of guys

At its worst, the crew is:

■ A dysfunctional family

■ Petty and small minded

■ Worried about personalities instead of the work

■ An ongoing power struggle

■ A bunch of minor-league dropouts

Your crew is your job-site family. I'm not saying you have to love them. You don't even have to like them. There will be people that get on your nerves. But there will also be people you like and respect. Either way, you have to work with them, so you might as well make the best of it. If your crew interacts with humor and brotherhood, life will be good. If there's nonstop conflict, it won't.

The Crew: Your Role

You can't control what other people do. You can only control yourself and your responses to them. What you bring to the crew can be positive or negative. It's always up to you. When I was on a crew, I was young and green. So I contributed by being the "do anything" guy. Shit jobs? No problem. Forgot something? I'll go get it. Something extra needed? I'll do it. Why? Because I wanted to be seen as a good guy who could be counted on. Even if I couldn't be the most skilled worker, I could still be useful as the "go-to" guy on the crew.

That kind of attitude earned me a lot of respect from day one. I'm sure that's how I earned leadership roles in almost every job I've ever had. It was always up to me. And I was never too important to do any job. Advice: be your own man (or woman) and chart your own course on the crew. It's up to nobody but you.

The Nifty Fifty

Here are fifty quick tips and reminders to help make you a more successful journeyman:

1. Gas up your car the night before work.
2. Never cash your check at a bar.
3. Don't burn bridges at any company.
4. Go to the doctor when you need to.
5. Earn respect (above all else).

6. Compliment co-workers when they deserve it.

7. Coach co-workers when they need it.

8. Quit smoking (or at least cut down).

9. Take advantage of any and all union-provided training.

10. Mentor an apprentice.

11. If you're an apprentice, find a mentor.

12. If you know this industry isn't for you, find something else that fits.

13. Clean up at the end of the shift, not twenty minutes early.

14. Do your share of shit work.

15. Learn people's names.

16. Know the boss's name, face, and truck.

17. Believe in yourself.

18. Eat breakfast.

19. Don't take a bad day on the job home with you.

20. Don't bring home issues to work.

21. If everybody at work hates you, get a dog.

22. More than one hangover a month on a workday is a bad sign.

23. Learn CPR.

24. Don't shortcut safety for production.

25. Don't shortcut quality for production.

26. Don't shortcut production for socializing.

27. Ask for more if you deserve it.

28. Push for foreman if you want it.

29. Learn your company's history.

30. Splurge for quality boots.
31. Drink tons of water when it's hot.
32. No horseplay.
33. Learn a couple of good jokes.
34. Don't lend your stuff.
35. Don't borrow stuff.
36. Don't lend money on the job.
37. Don't borrow money on the job.
38. Put things back.
39. Check the crew truck one more time to make sure you've got what you need.
40. Become friends with the dispatcher.
41. Be someone people look up to.
42. Never put yourself above others.
43. Go to union meetings.
44. Be proud of yourself.
45. Show up early.
46. Save up for something you really want and pay for it in cash.
47. Do something really nice for your spouse at least once a month.
48. Stand up for others on the job when it's right, even if it's unpopular.
49. Give this book to someone on your job site.
50. Make sure loving your kids is your first priority.
51. _____ (fill in your own).

Tolerance, Diversity and Attitude Adjustments

"Come on, we're all friends here.
Not to each other, but to someone."

—Unknown

Better Than Some, Worse Than Others

Unless God put a little gold plaque on your ass proclaiming you to be better than the rest of us, you probably aren't. Which means you've got no right to mess with anybody on the job because of their race, accent, gender, or anything else. Prejudice on the job is a waste of time and energy. If you have issues like this, leave them at home.

White, Black, Brown, or Green

Construction was a good old boys club for many years. Back in the day, if you weren't a white guy, you could forget about getting a union job. But now times have changed. Now most job sites have every race, ethnicity, and gender. Every one of us belongs. It doesn't matter if you're white, black, brown, or green. It doesn't matter if you are a guy or a gal.

What does matter is what kinds of skills and attitudes you bring. What matters is not *what* you are, but *who* you are. There are still some knuckle draggers out there. Guys who think all they have to do is act like prejudicial jerks and things will go back to "normal." If you're one of these guys, I hate to break it to you, but *you're* probably the one that doesn't belong anymore.

What If It Was You: **Prejudice** and **Stereotyping**

So let's say your favorite sports team decides they're going to start making assignments by race, religion, and nationality. Only white people are going to play key positions, only Protestants are going to start, and only native English speakers are going to pitch, kick, or shoot.

Pretty soon your team is in last place. They're the worst team in the league. Why? Duh! Because they stopped asking the most important question: who has what it takes to win? I don't mind rooting for a losing team, but I'm sure not gonna root for a stupid one.

Hola, Amigo?

More and more workers in the building trades are Hispanic (or Polish, Russian, and so on). It's just another step in our proud history of opportunity for the ones who have what it takes. Irish, Italian, Slavic, African American, and now Mexican and Eastern European—all of these groups have made up the bulk of the union construction workforce at one time or another. Bottom line: workforce makeup never stops changing.

By the way, knowing a little Spanish—or any other language used by folks on the job—is extremely valuable on the job site. Contractors are looking for foremen who can communicate with *all* the workers. Some even give Spanish classes after hours. Think about it.

Performance Profile: Susan Butcher

Title of Profile: **Toughest Competitor on the Planet (at 50° below)**

Name: Susan Butcher

Profile: Four-time winner of the Iditarod dog sled race in Alaska. One thousand two hundred miles, 24 hours a day. Minus 50+ degrees. Alone.

Key to Success: Grit, determination, no fear. Discount me because I'm a woman? See you at the finish line.

Backed It Up: Seven thousand two hundred miles. Four titles.

Lesson: A woman is one of the toughest competitors in the world, kicking ass and leaving no doubt.

Ladies, Start Your Engines

If you're a woman just starting out in construction, I'd like to extend a special welcome to you. You already know that you're entering what's still mostly a man's world. You know there'll be special challenges. More women are coming into construction every year. I hope things go smoothly for you, but there are bound to be a few rough spots. Here are a few issues you should think about so you'll be prepared:

1. You will be treated differently, and fitting in might not always be easy. This is not about you. It's about a lot of guys who have not spent much time with women on the job. Some of them will be uncomfortable at first. Don't worry; most will get over it eventually.

2. You're going to meet some sexist guys. There will be guys on the job who think they're God's gift to women. They will try to convince you of this.

3. It's possible that you'll be asked out or asked to get into some kind of relationship. Relationships involving co-workers at any workplace can cause problems (this goes for men and women). Especially if you break up and you're stuck working together. I know stuff happens, and you can't always stop it. Just think about how it might impact your job down the line is all I'm saying.

4. More than likely, you're eventually going to be hassled or harassed on a job site. It's wrong, and it needs to stop, but that doesn't mean it won't ever happen. Sooner or later somebody's going to cross the line. You'll need to

use your best judgment to deal with it. Don't let anybody mistreat or disrespect you. Every guy on that job has a mom. Most have a sister or a wife. They know right from wrong. Don't feel like you have to go along with it just to fit in.

Here's some basic advice:

- If you have a problem with a guy on the job, be direct. Tell him you're not interested and that you want to be left alone.
- Don't think it'll go away if you just wait it out.
- Don't be afraid to go to your foreman or steward.
- If it's the foreman who's harassing you, ask for the EEO officer or even the company owner.
- Always go to your union if it escalates to anything you consider serious.

Gentlemen, Show Respect

Times have changed. Women's roles have changed. Women have proven that they can perform as well as men in very difficult situations. Women now serve in active combat duty, something that was unimaginable just a couple of decades ago. And of course they're also doing all sorts of construction jobs.

Don't like it? Get over it. Women are here to stay, and they've had to work like hell to prove that they can hack it. A lot of these women have also come to construction because the pay is good and they've got mouths to feed, just like you and everybody else.

There are discrimination laws and policies that deal with bad behavior toward women on the job site. But the best way to deal with it is not to tolerate it in the first place. If your co-worker starts hassling a female co-worker, tell him to knock it off. Be the stand-up guy who does the right thing.

What If It Was You: Harassment on the Job

Let's say you get a call from your sister. She's crying because some guy at her office keeps harassing her. Saying sexually explicit things to her. Pushing her for a date. Won't take no for an answer. She says she doesn't know what to do. I don't know about you, but if it was me, that f---ker would be needing a good dentist.

Stick up for every woman (or anyone being mistreated due to race, creed, or gender) that ever comes on the job site. What if it was your sister? Wouldn't you want somebody to do the same thing for her?

Chapter Nine

Who Let the Dogs Out?

"I'm not loafing; I work so fast
that I'm always finished."

—Anonymous

Who Let The Dogs Out: The 10 Percenters

Some guys are not cutting it out there. They are not contributing to the fight for union construction. You know it and I know it. They probably know it, too, but they probably don't give it a second thought. Well, here are some questions you need to ask:

- What percentage of guys on the job are not really pulling their weight?
- What percentage are not living up to the "Union Yes" promise?
- What percentage are not bringing the right skills, attitudes, or behaviors to the job?

What I usually hear is, "at least 10 percent of the guys." These 10 percent guys are:

- Unskilled, selfish, impaired, or all of the above
- An obstacle to our competing and winning
- Anchors tied around our necks, pulling us under
- Killing us in the market every single day by breaking our promise of greater union value

What do you think would happen if 10 percent of McDonald's hamburgers made people puke? Or if 10 percent of Red Wing's boot heels fell off? Or if 10 percent of Trojans broke? That's right, they'd go right out of business. And since we are selling union construction as the best value for your money, these guys are really hurting us badly.

In case you're not sure how to spot these guys, let's do a quick survey:

The "I Got Mine" Guys

Some guys have the attitude that, "I got mine, so who cares?" That type of thinking is exactly how we lost the marketplace. Selfishness like that is why there are fewer and fewer guys getting their shot.

Now don't get me wrong. If a guy got his because he's the best worker on every job site, that's terrific, and he deserves it. But if a guy got his because the union contract and business agent are always there to protect his dead ass, well, that's a different story. *I Got Mine* is not how unions and this industry became great. You don't get yours because you're entitled to it. You get yours by *earning* it.

Know-it-Alls

Every job site has a know-it-all. And most of the time, it's not a foreman or supervisor. It's funny how the know-it-all is almost never chosen to lead. And there's a good reason for this. It's because 99 percent of the time he doesn't know what he's talking about.

It is amazing that you got this far in life without the know-it-all's advice. He'll still insist on giving you the benefit of his "wisdom." And the know-it-all has no use for anything you have to say. He always knows better, and believe me, he'll tell you so at every opportunity. He'll tell you why he should be foreman, why you're doing your job wrong, how the union is totally screwed up and on and on.

You need exactly five words to communicate with the

know-it-all: "why don't you shut up?" Maybe he'll take it personally, but so what? The know-it-all takes *everything* personally anyway. This is just one more guy looking to waste your time and exaggerate his inflated sense of self-importance.

"I'm Not Helping Somebody Take My Job"

In the old days, more experienced workers thought that if they taught the younger guys too much, the younger guys might take their jobs. Now it's different. If we don't pass on what we know, non-union workers will get all our jobs. Plus, who do you think is going to be paying into the pension and health and welfare funds when you're a bald, gray, toothless, grumpy old bastard?

Job Site Whiners

Whiners have problems. Lots of them, in fact. Life is *so* unfair, and they expect you to listen to them bellyache about it. Here's a news flash: complaining never got anything built, and non-stop bitching never improved anything.

These are the people who always see the glass as half empty. People like these are almost always unhappy. They can't face that fact, so they talk about everything and everybody else. They feed off negativity and look to get others into the same mindset.

My advice: Look for people on the job who are there because they want to be there.

Four Fingered Flip Off?

There are certain guys on the work site who think safety is uncool. They're too cool to wear goggles or hearing protection. They think tying off is for sissies. They ride in buckets and go into un-shored trenches, and they don't lock-out and block out. They're the ones who end up getting hurt. Or worse.

Twenty years in the business and, like everybody else, I've seen guys get injured, crippled, and even killed because of just one moment of stupidity. That's all it takes. One careless moment can take days, weeks, months, or even years of recovery. Or it can be all over, just like that.

Don't become a four-fingered macho man. I mean, what if you have to flip somebody off?

Loser #27: Workers' Compensation Scammers

Construction is hard, physical work. Even careful guys can get hurt. Or disabled. There's a system in place to take care of guys who get hurt on the job. It is called Workers' Compensation Insurance. It's set up to help anybody who gets hurt on the job. If you get hurt, Workers' Compensation pays your medical expenses, rehab, and whatever else you need. It's there to protect you.

Never let anybody talk you out of getting treatment if and when you need it. It's one of your basic rights on any job site. On the other hand, you'll meet guys who look at Workers' Comp as a free ride. They'll scam it by exaggerating minor injuries, taking time off when they don't need to, and filing claim after claim after claim.

Workers' Comp scammers hurt union construction. False claims raise the contractor's insurance costs. Dollars paid out for false claims end up coming out of the contractor's pocket and your future raises and benefits increases. The guy scamming the system is actually ripping us all off in the long run. Plus, Workers' Comp costs are based on how much a contractor pays per hour. If his Comp premiums go up, it's harder for him to compete with non-union contractors and their lower paid workers. It's a double whammy.

Besides all the cost and competitiveness issues, scamming Workers' Comp is just plain wrong. What kind of man goes off to work in the morning thinking, *how can I scam the system today*? A man with self-respect doesn't pull that kind of penny-ante crap. Bottom line: Use Workers' Comp when you need it and in the right way.

Job Site **Politicians**

Somebody wants your vote. He's running for Most Important Guy on the job site. This guy spends a lot of time campaigning. The trouble is, all the time he spends trying to boost his self-image is time he could be spending doing productive work. He's always looking for others who'll listen to him and make him feel important.

Job site politicians are insecure. They need constant approval. They're trying to get it on the job, and they're selfish about it. Don't give them your vote. Vote for yourself and your future instead. Suggest to The Candidate that he go look for somebody who cares.

Chapter Ten

For Apprentices Only

"Making a success of the job you've got is the best step toward the job you want."

—B. Baruch

Performance Profile: Rookies of the Year

Title of Profile: **Rookies of the Year**

(Some) Names:
1947—Jackie Robinson, MLB
1951—Willie Mays, MLB
1959—Wilt Chamberlin, NBA
1963—Pete Rose, MLB
1968—Johnny Bench, MLB
1970—Lew Alcindor (Kareem Abdul-Jabbar), NBA
1972—Franco Harris, NFL
1977—Tony Dorsett, NFL
1981—Fernando Valenzuela, MLB
1984—Patrick Ewing, NBA
1997—Allan Iverson, NBA
1992—Shaquille O'Neil, NBA
1993—Mike Piazza, MLB
1994—Marshall Faulk, NFL
2002—Ilya Kovalchuk, NHL
2003—LeBron James, NBA

Profile: Best of the new guys

Key to Success: High achievement from moment one. No waiting around to hit high gear. Stepped up and contributed at the highest level as fast as they could.

Backed it Up: All went on from Rookies of the Year (apprentices) to become superstars and legends.

Lesson: Go for it early.

Apprentices: Welcome to Our World, ROOKiE

I'd like to extend a big welcome to all the apprentices reading this book. Welcome to a fun, challenging, rewarding career. How you got here is not as important as what you do with the opportunity. To help make things easier, I've created this chapter just for you.

The PROViNG Grounds

The beginning of your career is about proving yourself on the job site. Don't expect to be welcomed with open arms. Some guys are not going to be glad to see you. They'll see you as somebody who doesn't get it. They'll see you as somebody who just gets in the way of getting the job done.

Don't let these guys discourage you. They think you ask too many questions? Be sure to ask the right ones. They think you're there to take their job? Let them know how much you appreciate their help. Some guys will understand that you are the future. They'll take the time to help you succeed. In the meantime, watch, listen, and make yourself useful.

Day **One** Through Year **One**

Your first year in the craft is a make-or-break proposition. Many union apprenticeship programs have a 10-20 percent or higher dropout rate. Here are some of the reasons that guys don't make it through the first year:

- Didn't understand what they were getting into
- Didn't have a stable home life
- Transportation problems
- Missed training classes because they couldn't deal with schooling
- Hard partying lifestyle conflicted with work and studying
- Thought they could beat the drug test
- Didn't manage their money well
- Didn't realize how hard they'd have to work
- Didn't like being told what to do

Take a hard look at each of these. If you see yourself in any of them, I'd advise you to think about your decision carefully. Becoming a union craftsperson is an outstanding opportunity *if it's right for you*. If not, like I said before, there's no shame in doing something else.

We don't need folks who just want a job. We need people who are fired up and who understand that they'll have to jump through some hoops along the way. We want you to succeed, but we can't do it for you.

No Babysitting Provided

The union isn't a babysitting service. They're not there to carry dead weight. They're not there to coddle you. Unions exist to uphold high standards of excellence. They exist to provide opportunities. They exist to create power through solidarity.

Unions promote fairness and equality in return for your effort and commitment. The union is not your big brother. It's not going to protect you when you do something stupid, reckless or dishonest. Union people are professionals who are there to represent other professionals.

Apprentice Hazing: Hang Tough

Sooner or later (most likely sooner), you're bound to meet a few guys who think you're there for their amusement. Guys who are going to give you a hard time because you're an apprentice. These guys will test you. They'll push you. They might even insult you or abuse you a little.

Just remember this: Jerks that pick on new guys are the exception, not the rule in this industry. Don't let them get to you. Just hang tough and let 'em know you're not there to take any crap. Eventually they'll get the message. And remember, when you become a journeyman, protect that new apprentice. Don't coddle him, but at least help make sure he gets a fair shake.

Peer Pressure

When you're new on a job site, there will be a lot of personalities to deal with. Anytime you come in cold like that, you'll face some peer pressure. This can be good, or it might be bad. Just keep in mind that picking up bad habits and attitudes just to fit in is never a good idea. Maybe you won't always be able to do or say what you want. The key is to avoid bad habits. All that does is create an even more negative atmosphere for the next crop of new guys.

They'll Love You or Hate You

People on the job site are either going to love you or hate you. If you make yourself useful and look for something to do every minute, you'll be loved and respected. Bust ass all the time for everybody, and the crew will notice. On the other hand, if you stand around a lot like a dumb rookie, you won't be too popular. It's pretty simple.

And Many will Fall

You'll see many folks fall by the wayside. Here's how it usually breaks down:

- 20+ percent of apprentices will eventually drop out or get canned
- Another 10+ percent of journeymen will drop out in their first five years.

The industry, life's choices, and random chance sort out everybody's place. Remember, don't take the opportunity for granted. A lot of guys who thought they were going to make it in this industry didn't make it. Whatever the reason, don't let it happen to you. Pay attention. Be smart. Make good choices, for many will fall.

Buy Once, Buy Quality

When you're an apprentice, it can be hard to pay for top quality work tools and clothes. Still, you're always better off buying the best stuff, even if it costs more. Get into the habit of paying for quality, and it'll serve you well. Carhartt and DeWalt are like union construction: they cost more, but they're worth it because they're a better value.

Living on That **Shoestring**

An apprentice doesn't make much. "First you learn, then you earn" is the way it works. The contractor and the union spend a lot of money training you over the course of several years. You're an investment. When that investment starts paying off, you both benefit. That's why you don't get paid much at first. It can make things tough over the first couple of years, especially if you have a family.

Here are ten rules for good apprentice money management:

1. Remember that our work is seasonal; you can't count on a 40-hour paycheck year-round.

2. Save something for when you're not working. Vacation pay is not enough. Fifty bucks a week is a minimum. A hundred is even better.

3. Don't worry about the toys just yet. You don't need a new F-150 payment. You don't need a bass boat payment. Or an ATV. Or a Harley. Don't worry, these things will come soon enough. Look around at successful guys in the trades. Lots of them have all the toys. Smart ones have rental houses and country property. Guys who are spending every dollar, every week, every year never get there.

4. Don't blow out your credit cards.

5. Have two bank accounts, one for savings with a *do-not-touch* sign on it and a checking account for bills.

6. Don't piss away your paycheck. Never cash your check at a bar or check-cashing center. Cash in the pocket tends

to disappear quickly. Deposit your check to your bank account. Direct deposit is even better, if it's available.

7. Keep your vehicle well maintained. An ounce of prevention is worth a pound of cure. A new engine, transmission, or U-joints can put a serious dent in your cash flow.

8. Stay healthy. If you don't take care of your body it won't take care of you.

9. Take the overtime if you can get it. Some guys don't want to work OT. Just remember, it won't always be there, and those extra dollars add up quickly.

10. When you get to be a journeyman, making good money, live like you're still an apprentice. Then when you want that toy or trip you'll have the cash to do it.

Study Up on Your **Fringe** Benefits

Your fringe benefits come to between $6 and $12 for every hour you work. That's a lot of moolah. Most non-union guys don't get anything close to that. It just makes sense that you understand what your benefits are, how they work, and what you'll be earning over time.

Being a union worker is a great deal. But some guys only look at what goes in their pockets each week. Study up on these basic benefits issues:

Health Benefit Plan—How does it work? How many hours do I need to qualify for it and maintain it? What is a bank of hours? How does my family use it?

Pension—How do pension credits accumulate? What will my projected pension be at 5, 10, and 20 years? Do I qualify for pensioned health and welfare (partial payment of health premiums) for when I am old and gray?

Credit Union—Do I have access to an affiliated credit union? Do they have a better deal on credit card interest and loans?

Annuities—What are they and why should I care?

Life is not only about next payday. If you have kids and/or retirement plans, you know what I mean. I didn't have any kind of pension program until I was almost 30 (dumb!). I wish I'd followed the advice I'm giving you. Understand how it works for you now and in the future. Because the future has a way of sneaking up on you.

Back in the Classroom

Apprentice classes are not always fun, and that's putting it mildly. First you have to do 40+ hours of work per week, and then you have to go to apprentice school on top of it? Ouch.

I know that a lot of you were never too excited about sitting in a classroom. I know it's sometimes boring as hell. But you need to learn as much as possible as fast as possible. And the stuff you learn in class is directly related to how successful you're going to be (and how much money you're going to make) for the next 20 years.

Dropping out is not an option, so why not make the best of it? And that guy next to you who's sleeping or doodling in class? You can be damn sure he's not going to make the cut when it comes down to the Survival of the Fittest.

The Training Center——What a Deal

The union training center is one of the best investments the union makes, and it's one of the best benefits you can get as a member. It's amazing to me that not every member takes advantage of it. Believe me, even though there aren't that many outstanding deals in life, this is one of them. The reason is simple: the better trained you are, the more you're worth.

The training center is about lifting people up. It's about making better men and women. You might take it for granted, but when you think about it, the training center is an incredibly valuable benefit. Use it!

The Training Staff

If you want to see the most under-appreciated guys in our business, it's the training center staff. These are the guys *creating* the skilled people to drive our industry forward, but they usually don't get the recognition they deserve.

The training staff isn't there because they've got nothing better to do; they do it because they're committed to helping people and helping our industry. They could be doing regular construction jobs instead of dealing with a bunch of knot-heads and smart-asses, and they could probably be making more money in the bargain. So give them a little respect and consideration. Pay attention to what they have to say, and 5, 10, or 15 years from now you'll be glad you did.

Steel, Iron, Wood . . . and Microchips?

Do your kids know way more than you do about computers and technology? You're not alone. My daughter has never even known a world without cell phones. Being a blue-collar worker used to mean your tools were made of steel and wood. Not anymore. Take lasers, for example. They used to be in sci-fi movies and comic books. Now they're on every job site. Take advantage of every chance to learn about technology because that is the direction of our industry. If you don't understand something, you can always ask your kids for help.

Big Companies vs. Small Companies

For a new guy, what are the benefits of working for different types and sizes of companies? Let's take a quick look. When you're working for a big company, there are certain advantages:

- More area covered = more job opportunities
- Better training programs
- More opportunity to move up to lead man or supervisor
- Opportunity to learn how large companies are organized and managed
- Easier to find a mentor

There are disadvantages, too:

- Don't feel like part of the company

■ Don't know the owner or boss
■ Feel like a cog in the machine

What about small company advantages?
■ Do a little of everything
■ More of a family atmosphere
■ Know the owner personally
■ Feel more appreciated

Possible downsides include:
■ More limited training opportunities
■ More vulnerable to the company's financial problems
■ Less opportunity for advancement

Chapter Eleven

Security, Stability, and the Money Game

"Money isn't everything—but it is a long way
ahead of what comes next."

—E. Stockdale

Being Financially Responsible

Money management can be a real challenge for people in our business. At a regular job, you work forty hours week year-round. You work and get the check no matter what season or what type of weather. In construction it's different. You might be busting your butt all summer, then barely working at all in winter.

Plenty of guys make the mistake of thinking (and spending like) the paycheck they're getting when it's busy is going to be the paycheck they can expect every single week. Here are three useful suggestions:

1. Plan for downtime and remember that vacation pay usually will not cover all your expenses.

2. Try not to live paycheck to paycheck. Toys are nice, but they can become a financial ball and chain if you're not careful.

3. If you get stuck in the "budget gap," don't ignore it, and don't lean on credit cards more than you have to.

Having a good life means being financially responsible. Money doesn't buy happiness, but *lack* of money can definitely make you miserable. Money stress is the worst kind because it just sits on you day after day. It can kill marriages. It can start the booze or drug downhill slide. It can suck all the joy right out of life. Sometimes you're just unlucky, and there's nothing you can do about it. But if you're pulling down halfway decent money and still not getting by, something's wrong.

If you don't know how to budget and save, start learning.

There are tons of books on personal finance. Read a couple of them. There are classes and personal finance counselors, too. Bottom line: take care of your money so it'll be there to take care of you.

Credit Cards: The Bottomless Pit

Let's keep this real simple:

- Buy what you *need*
- Save for what you *want*
- Don't buy what you can't afford
- If you can't pay for it now, what makes you think you can pay for it later?
- A credit card is not real money

Any questions?

In Over Your Head

A lot of folks put off dealing with their financial problems until they're in over their heads. More than 20 percent of union construction workers are getting their wages garnished—money taken out of their paychecks by court order—to pay off their debts, taxes, credit cards, child support, or similar.

It's always better to deal with a problem early than wait until you're overwhelmed. If you're in over your head, contact a credit counseling service immediately. Ask your credit union to refer you to a good one.

Little Things Add Up

Let's take a look at a few other examples of little things that take a bite out of your earnings:

Coffee and Donuts	$2.00 per day	$10 per week	$500 per year
Lunch	$7.00 per day	$35 per week	$1750 per year
Gas (two gallons)	$5.00 per day	$25 per week	$1250 per year
Smokes (pack a day)	$4.00 per day	$28 per week	$1450 per year

TOTAL: $4950 per year

Let's think about these numbers. By eating breakfast at home, brown bagging your lunch, car-pooling and giving up smoking (or going to half a pack), you'll save around three and a half or four grand a year. And of course, this is *after tax* money we're talking about, which means you have to earn around six grand to pay for all this stuff to begin with.

The little things add up. Fast. If you were to save most of the money that slips away every week, you could afford a new truck payment. Or boat payment. Or summer cabin payment. Or you could have a nice vacation every year. Think about where it goes because it disappears fast when you're not paying attention.

Million Dollar Blue Collar

How fast does your money add up?

$55,000* per year x 5 years = $225,000

$55,000 per year x 10 years = $550,000

$55,000 per year x 15 years = $775,000

$55,000 per year x 20 years = $1,050,000

*Average yearly career earnings

You're going to be making that million dollars. Whether you have anything to show for it 10, 15, or 20 years down the road is up to you.

Chapter Twelve

For Foremen Only

"A leader is one who knows the way, goes the way, and shows the way."

— John Maxwell

For Foremen Only

The foreman may very well be the key to the whole union construction industry. No single individual has a greater impact on our competitive situation every day. Motivation, leadership, production, and profit—they're all in the foreman's hands.

In this section we'll cover:

- What a foreman is
- What a foreman is not
- What a foreman does
- What a foreman doesn't do

The Money Maker

The foreman is the most important person on the job as far as making or losing money. The foreman is the one who determines how the job gets done. A good foreman can take a bad job and turn it around. A lousy foreman can take a sweet job and ruin it. A good foreman can do great work even with a weak crew. A bad one can have all superstars and still screw things up. Everything and everyone on the job are influenced by the foreman.

Leading by Example

A crew will only work as hard as the foreman does. Some foremen think their only job is to tell people what to do. Their real job is to lead by example and demonstrate how to do things the right way. If they succeed, they'll command authority and respect. If not, they won't.

The Mentor and Coach

The foreman's most important job is to get the best effort from every worker. Like any good coach, you have to be able to read people. You have to understand what motivates them. You have to deal with their personal problems. You have to use your head, and sometimes your heart. You have to develop confidence and skill in every worker. You have to develop their loyalty and respect for you and the company. It's powerful stuff…if you do it right.

The Paperwork King

One of the toughest things about moving up to foreman is the paperwork. It's not enough to be a master craftsman and a leader of men. If the job gets messed up because you can't handle the paperwork, trouble will follow. Even time cards can be a pain in the ass. Still, it's all necessary. A good foreman has to be organized with the paperwork.

The Yelling Idiot

"You can't raise a man up by calling him down."
—W. Boetcker

Nobody likes being yelled at. A good foreman might do it from time to time just to wake somebody up. But yelling all day, every day is not the mark of a good leader. You cannot motivate people by yelling at them constantly. If you do, you'll lose their respect and motivate them only out of fear. Again, not the best way to get your people's best effort.

A Professional, Not a Pal

It's not the foreman's job to be anybody's buddy. The foreman's primary role is to get the job done. Maybe he won't always be the most well liked person, but that doesn't matter. What does matter is that the foreman commands respect. It's about pushing the job. It's about being focused and professional. If you're friends with the foreman, don't expect preferred treatment. The minute a foreman starts playing favorites, he's in big trouble.

The Foreman who Plays Favorites

Everybody has friends on the job site, but the foreman who plays favorites is doing nobody a favor. Playing favorites always hurts morale big-time. Plus, when others see the foreman's buddies getting away with stuff, they're going to lose all motivation to do their best work. Pretty soon, the foreman loses all credibility, and the job goes right down the toilet. I've seen it happen.

If the contractor finds out that some guys are getting preferential treatment, there is definitely going to be hell to pay. Treat everybody according to their performance and attitude. If you're friends with some of the workers, be upfront with them. Tell them you have to treat everybody on the job exactly the same. No special favors. They should understand and respect you for it.

Ten Tips for Being a Great Foreman

1. Remember that your actions are more important that your words.
2. Make sure the work and materials are pre-planned so the job keeps moving.
3. Be responsible for everyone's safety. No compromises.
4. Treat the company's money like it's your own.
5. Treat your crew like they're your own kids.
6. Use praise as a motivator.
7. Remember that loyalty comes from trust and respect.

8. Don't talk negatively about anybody in front of other workers.

9. Don't ask your crew to do anything that you wouldn't do yourself.

10. Jump in and help the crew on something extra hard or nasty once in a while.

Ten Tips for Being a Lousy Foreman

1. Act like you're better than everybody else.
2. Show up late and/or leave early.
3. Cut corners on safety to boost production .
4. Treat people without dignity or respect.
5. Have an attitude about gender or color.
6. Don't teach anybody anything.
7. Be dishonest.
8. Waste materials, lose paperwork, and make excuses.
9. Play favorites with your buddies.
10. Get fired without seeing it coming.

Getting Involved On and Off the Job

"A working class hero is something to be."

—John Lennon

An **Invitation** to Leadership

One of the many great things about this business is that you don't need a formal education to move up. Your ability to become a "lead man," foreman, superintendent, or even contractor is limited only by your own vision and desire.

If you're thinking about moving up to a leadership role, here are 10 skills you should think about working on:

1. Mastery of your craft
2. Communication (verbal and written)
3. Reading blueprints and plans
4. Job planning and scheduling
5. Organizational skills and habits
6. Time management
7. Motivation
8. Diplomacy
9. Safety management
10. Computer, e-mail, and Internet

You don't have to be an expert at everything, but you cannot get along without a little bit of each. There are plenty of good management books out there. Your union probably has supervision courses. Take them every time.

Be a **Mentor**

If you're a journeyman, you have the opportunity to help keep union construction strong by mentoring the next generation. Passing along knowledge and skills is what the apprenticeship system is all about. It is also about being a good person.

Mentoring is not about giving someone the skills they need to take your job. Your fellow workers are not the competition. Non-union construction is the competition, and we've let them get way too strong. When you help out the guy working next to you, you're helping to grow *the pie* so we can all get what we want and need. The better we all are, the better off you will be personally.

Passing it Along: The Vanishing Craft Masters

There's a whole generation of craft "masters" getting ready to retire. Unfortunately, they haven't always been open to passing on their expertise. They're a vanishing resource, and we need to encourage them to share what they know before they hang up their tools for good.

The average age in many unions is over 45 years old. Who's going to replace these guys as they age out? The older guys are one of the most important resources we'll ever have. If you're one of them, please consider helping out the younger people coming up.

If you're just starting out, try like hell to get one of these masters to take you under his wing. Help him out. Offer to carry his tools or get his coffee. It'll be well worth it, believe me.

Moving up in Your Union

A tiny percentage of union members attend meetings. An even smaller percentage serve as executive board members or in other positions. It's easy to see why: it's time away from family and hobbies. But it's not a *waste* of time. The well being of the union movement is based 100 percent on the right people leading.

Why not you? If you're:

■ Interested in challenging yourself

■ Interested in developing your leadership ability

■ Committed to positive change

■ A good communicator

■ A great example on the job site

■ A leader and a motivator

…think about serving as a union leader. Don't do it if you want power over others, or if you think you can use it for your own personal gain, or if you just don't believe things can get better. Do it with a positive attitude and make a difference.

Steward

Let's look at the construction steward's role and responsibilities. The steward looks out for the interests of workers on the job site. The steward makes sure:

- Small problems and issues are resolved
- Small problems don't become big ones
- No one gets screwed
- There's always a union representative available to workers

Back in the 1960s and 70s, some unions and stewards took the role a little too far. More than a few contractors and project owners quit being union because of problems with stewards on power trips. What kinds of problems? Let's just put it under the category of *Things Not to Do as a Union Steward*:

- Don't create problems where there aren't any
- Don't make promises you can't keep
- Don't back guys that are clearly dishonest
- Don't go on a power trip
- Don't look at the contractor as your enemy
- Don't dog it on the job because you're the steward
- Don't act like you can't be fired (you can!)

A good steward focuses on:

- Addressing worker problems quickly and effectively
- Making sure the job site is safe for every worker
- Resolving issues that don't need to become grievances

■ Communicating with the business agent and contractor when necessary.

The steward should be a great example and a good leader, and should know how to get along with people. Know anybody who fits the bill?

Red, White, and Blue collar Voter

Around 35 percent of your money goes to taxes. That's roughly equal to all the money you make in January, February, March, and April. With the government taking that much dough, you might as well have some say in how it's spent. It's called voting.

I know most guys in the business don't care about politics. I myself have a pretty low opinion of most politicians, and I've met more than a few. The problem is that they control public money and policy and all kinds of stuff that affects us every day. It's not just some theoretical crap on CNN. It's an important part of our democratic life in North America. And your union is counting on you to understand that your own wallet depends on it.

A lot of people think, *what does my one little vote matter*? That's why most people don't even bother. Let me tell why it does matter. Believe it or not, different candidates do have different ideas on how your money gets spent. Take the time to learn what your local government is up to. If somebody's running for city council that wants to build a new civic center, well, it sounds like a lot of union construction work might be coming to your neighborhood. That candidate might be worth voting for.

National politics affects your life, too. Find out who supports union labor; it's not always obvious. No matter who's in office, get into the habit of calling or writing them to say what you like and don't like about what they're doing with *your money*. If you don't speak up, they'll figure you don't care. If you do speak up, they'll know you do.

I'm not telling you how to vote. You have to vote your own convictions. It's your right and responsibility. *How* involved you get is up to you. Just don't be indifferent about it. It's your money, your opportunity, and your vote.

Chapter Fourteen

Old Enemies, New Partners

"People who work together will win, whether it be against complex football defenses or the problems of modern society."

—Vince Lombardi

Enemies No More: Doing **the Threesome**

Hey, hey…don't get too excited about the title; I'm not talking about *that* kind of threesome. I'm talking about the three-way partnership that keeps your paychecks coming every month. Here's what it looks like:

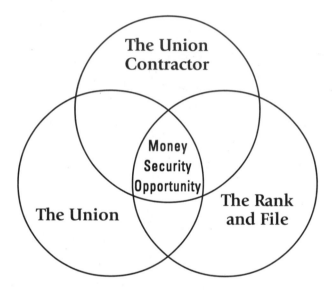

1. The Union Contractor
2. The Union
3. The Rank and File

Each of these three plays a crucial role in the partnership. Each one has to contribute, or the partnership breaks down. Here are the key functions:

The Union **Contractor**

- Finds the work
- Takes the financial risk
- Buys the equipment and materials
- Signs the union agreements
- Deals with owners, agencies, and developers
- Signs and pays the bills
- Helps market the partnership
- Deals with most of the headaches

The **Union**

- Recruits the best workers
- Invests in ongoing worker training and productivity enhancement
- Operates a dispatch and referral system
- Represents the workers' best interests
- Administers workers' benefits
- Helps market the partnership

The Rank and File

- Provides the highest quality end product
- Maintains and improves the union's reputation
- Makes the contractor the most competitive
- Provides the best value for the construction dollar

If any of the partners fail to hold up their end of the bargain, the business model falls apart. Without a competitive union contractor, there's no work. Without the union, there's no recruitment, no training, and no workers. And without the *best* union workers, the entire union concept becomes meaningless and everything goes non-union.

In the old days, labor and management were enemies. Not anymore. Now we've finally figured out that the best way to prosper is by working *with* each other instead of being at each other's throats. It's a team dedicated to the Survival of the Fittest.

The **BOSS** as **Bad** Guy?

The contractor is just a rich guy.
The contractor is a heartless jerk.
The contractor is the enemy.

You've probably heard some of this if you've been on a job site for more than a few years. But as you probably know, the contractor is more and better than that. He was probably a lot like you when he started out. He was ambitious and hard working, and he was willing to risk it all.

Remember, he didn't win the Lotto to get where he is; he worked for it. While you're enjoying your morning coffee, he's already worrying about having enough men and materials to get the day's work done. While you're tossing back a cold one after your shift, he's still planning the next day's work.

So who is *the contractor*?

- The guy who had the courage to risk everything
- The guy who will lose everything if things go bad
- The guy who has a three-out-of-five chance of going broke in his first five years
- The only guy on the job site whose work *always* goes home with him
- The guy whose success your job depends on, tomorrow, next week, next year
- The guy who's not so different from you (even if he does have a nicer truck).

Contractors—Regular Guys Done Good

On a lot of jobs you never even see the contractor or owner. So people get an idea of who he or she is without really knowing them. I'd like to introduce you to some successful union contractors I've known:

- Steve used to work at a NAPA Auto Parts counter. He was the first guy hired by a small contractor. Had a high school education. Spent 20 years working his way up from field to office. Now he runs the company. They did $80 million last year. He likes to fish for steelhead.

- Mike was a high school dropout. Started as a backhoe operator and part-time drag racer. Still drives a pick up and wears cowboy boots. Has 300 guys in the field today. Owns a racing team.

- Dave started out driving a truck and delivering stuff. Has a nice small company with one crew. Everybody's like family. They've all been together for at least ten years. Almost went broke twice on bad jobs. He's got a bad stomach.

- M.C. has had ADD (attention deficit disorder) since he was a kid. Got kicked out of a bunch of schools. Went to work in the field for a big company. Took advantage of every training opportunity they had. Started his own company. Built it up. Works in six states. Has a nice fishing boat. Hates golf.

- Bob was a long-haired, Harley-riding brawler. He's also the smartest person I've ever met. He put it to work. Ran $30 million jobs while he was still in his twenties.

Built two companies doing more than $100 million each. Believes in union construction more than anybody I've ever met.

■ Joe's a second-generation contractor. Used his money to adopt 15 minority kids and provide emergency shelter for more than 1000 others over 20 years.

■ Juan came here from Mexico illegally. He's legal now and pays more in taxes than most of us make. On his way up, he almost went broke three times.

■ Dave worked on the Alaska Pipeline. Came home and started his own business. Had a bad job and then another. Went broke (not every story has a happy ending!).

I've known these guys personally for many years. The thing is, there's no one kind of contractor. Nobody gets there without paying some serious dues. Nobody gets there without guts and determination. Some win big. Some lose big. But they're definitely not all a bunch of stuck-up, golf-playing, Mercedes-driving jerk-offs. Far from it. Lesson: *Don't assume you know anything about a man just because his title is "boss."*

The Union's **Key** Role

What does the union do in the partnership? It represents you, manages your benefits, negotiates your contracts, and a whole lot more. A key role for the union is using business agents and organizers to line up more union contractors and more jobs. This is probably the union's most important job: Creating *your* next job.

The **Business** Agent's Role (Do I Want **That** Guy's Job?)

Who is the business agent? At first glance, it looks like a pretty easy deal. The business agent gets to work off the job site. He has a car. He seems to spend a lot of time schmoozing. Sound pretty good? OK, let's say you get hired as a business agent. Here's what you get to do:

- Be on call all the time. Watching Monday Night Football, and somebody's wife calls asking about benefits? Suck it up 'cause it's part of your job.
- Deal with some of the worst guys in the union. The troublemakers. The big mouths. The crybabies. In fact, you get to spend *most* of your time dealing with them. Oh, and they talk smack about you anyway. Still sound good?
- Work nights
- Have everybody (contractors and rank and file) criticize you all the time

■ Be ready to get kicked out or voted out anytime

The business agent's job is not easy. But it directly affects your employment. Here's some of what they do for you:

■ Grow the pie by getting non-union contractors to do business with the union

■ Take care of *real* problems and make sure the members are well represented

■ Represent the union with local politicians who decide who gets work in the future

■ Build better relationships with existing union contractors to improve your working conditions

■ Negotiate better terms, conditions, and wages

■ Represent your interests in legitimate grievances

Give the business agent a break. You may not always see it, but he's probably doing the best he can. If you think you can do a better job, go for it. Just don't say I didn't warn you how tough and often thankless a job it really is.

The **Rank** and **File's** Key **Role**

The rank and file are really the most important piece of the puzzle. It's up to you, every single day on the job, to demonstrate that the union workforce really is the best value. If we all work together on this, we'll all get more of what we want and need. Nobody's going to hand it to us on a platter, that's for sure.

Organizing is About **Growing the Pie**

With all this talk about "organizing" and "growing the pie," you're probably saying, *who cares? Why should we bring in guys who probably aren't as good as me? Or, even worse, what if they* are *as good and I have to compete for the next job?*

Growing the pie and organizing is a little more complicated than that. Here are a few things to think about:

1. More union contractors means more union jobs. That's why organizing non-union companies is so important.

2. We need to offer an unbeatable value. As we talked about before, we have a great product to sell. If we can't provide it, we can't sell it, and if we can't sell it, we can't grow. If we can't grow, we can't ask for what we want from the contractors at the bargaining table.

3. Newly converted non-union workers are not the enemy. Some guys say, *hey, this guy is just competing for my job.* Duh. He was already competing for your job as a non-union worker. And for less money. What would you rather have, an equal playing field, or some guy undercutting you?

Everybody has a role in organizing.

Front Door Organizing—A Crazy Idea

If you've attended *COMET* or other programs that help the union organize new members, here's a crazy idea: Instead of just sending guys in through the back door as salts, why not also send them through the front door as superstars?

A non-union contractor is a person that hasn't been convinced yet that we're the best in the world. How are we going to change their minds? Think of four guys in your local union that are the real thing. I mean everybody knows that these guys are the cream of the crop.

What if we were to send those four guys to a non-union job site and show the non-union contractor what he's missing? By the end of the day, he should be so impressed that he'll be ready to sign a union contract on the spot. On the other hand, if the four guys aren't way better than his non-union guys, why should he sign?

Here's the key: *You* should be one of those four guys. Any union worker should be able to work circles around any non-union worker. If we make twice what they make, our productivity and quality should be at least two times better than theirs. Even though we cost more, we should still be a bargain.

I hope you're ready to walk through that door to prove it, because we're going to need your help.

Who Are These **Assholes?** (And Other Frequently Asked Questions on Organizing)

A lot of guys figure it's a bad idea to organize these non-union workers. We hear stuff like:

"Why do we need these guys when we already got enough guys in the union?"

"I don't want to compete with these guys for the next job."

"These guys aren't good enough. They don't belong."

"These guys didn't have to go through the apprenticeship program like me."

"Who are these assholes anyway?"

Here's a quick economics lesson: if some guy charges less than you do, people are going to want to hire him. Unless you can prove you're that much better. And even then, that lower cost thing is hard to ignore.

Bottom line: we can have them on the inside working with us or on the outside working against us. *They're going to be doing the work anyway.* If they're non-union, they have a cost advantage. Wouldn't you be better off with a level playing field instead of running uphill all the time?

It's not an easy call. But if we're going to move toward that 90 percent union market share we talked about earlier, we have to take in five-to-seven new union members for every existing union member. We need these people if we're going to grow our market and our unions. It's obviously more important to add new contractors. They employ the members and sign the union contracts. But eventually, we're going to need a whole lot more workers, too.

Scabs, Rats, and Other Future Friends

If I asked you for two words that describe non-union contractors and workers, what would they be? "Rat" and "Scab," maybe? These are words that have been used for decades. Well it is true that some contractors are unethical, cheating, lying SOBs. But there are plenty of non-union contractors that aren't. What if we thought of non-union contractors as "potential clients" instead of "rats"?

We need a little different attitude toward non-union contractors and non-union workers. We can't just look at them as rats, scabs, and competition. We have to look at (some of) them as future partners.

The non-union contractors are the main target. We need them, and we need them bad. They're a *huge* opportunity. They're the main way we're going to grow our market. We have to convince them that we represent an outstanding business proposition instead of simply picketing and boycotting them. Unions will have to use every tool possible to get their attention, but as businessmen they'll always pay attention to bottom-line results.

Life Success— You Are Worth It

"Life is like a grindstone.
Whether it grinds you down or polishes you up
depends on what you're made of."

—Unknown

Being Happy with Your Work

Everybody deserves to be happy. Like it or not, you're going to spend most of your life at work. You should have a sense of pride and accomplishment about the work you do. Otherwise, why bother? Hey, a paycheck is a paycheck; what's really important is how you earn it. Be happy about the good things in your life. Look at your job as *your* place to achieve something and grow your knowledge.

It's true that nobody can decide to be happy for you. Not every day will be daisies and sunshine. But even when you have an off day, try to see the bigger picture of your life and the good things your work brings to it.

So What If You Didn't Go To College?

A lot of guys in the industry might look down on themselves because they weren't so great in school. Well I'm here to tell you that it doesn't matter anymore. I'm not saying education isn't important; what I'm saying is that education isn't something you only get in a classroom.

There are plenty of college-educated idiots and just as many non-college educated geniuses. If you take a college graduate and a blue-collar guy and put them in any work situation, their success will depend on a number of things that have nothing to do with how many years they went to school. For example:

- Are they good with people?
- Do they follow through?
- Are they honest and ethical?
- Do they communicate well?
- Do they understand the business they're in?
- Are they focused and determined to succeed?
- Are they trying to improve themselves?
- Can they mentor others?
- Are they self-motivated?
- Can they lead?

I could write a whole book about dropouts who took the world by storm. Guys who figured their time was too valuable to waste on more school.

Example: Ray Kroc was a high school dropout. He built McDonald's into the most successful fast food restaurant chain in the world. Died a mega-millionaire. His widow gives millions to charity every year.

Example: Bill Gates was a college dropout. He built Microsoft from nothing and developed the software that powers 90 percent of the world's personal computers. Oh, and he's also worth about forty billion.

I could write a whole book about college graduates who couldn't tie your shoes. Give yourself some credit. Success is not just about what you know; it's about who you are. Know that you are the best in the world at what you do and start believing it today.

A Life in Balance

A guy once told me that if you dread going to work in the morning, then your life is pretty bad. And if you feel the same way about going back home at night, then you're really in trouble. So what do you do about it? You make sure your life is in balance. Don't worry, I'm not going *Dr. Phil* on you here, I'm just talking about making sure:

- You're having *fun* regularly
- You're working on the important relationships in your life
- You're taking time for yourself (but not being totally selfish about it)
- You're taking care of your health
- You're doing the things in this book to secure your future
- You're taking the time to involve yourself in your kids lives
- You're learning something new every month
- _____ (fill in your blank)

You know what you need better than I do. Just remember, too much of anything can mess up your life. *Not enough* of some things can also be a problem. Don't settle for less in your life. Your life is waiting for you right now. Take care of it. It's the only one you've got and the meter is running.

The Rut

OK, I know some of you are in *the Rut*. When you're in *the Rut*, everything sucks. It used to be fun and interesting, but now it's just painful. The job is a ball and chain, and it takes everything you've got to drag your butt out of bed and face the day.

I get it. Everybody hits *the Rut* once in a while. A lot of things can put you in *the Rut*:

- Long term unemployment
- Recovering from injury, or having a chronic injury
- Tough life issues: death / divorce / money problems
- Bored with life
- Depression
- Not feeling challenged
- Wondering if you made the right career choice
- Envious of others
- Booze/drugs
- _____ (fill in the blank)

I've even been there myself. After I got divorced, I was dragging for almost six months. Everybody I worked with knew I was bummed out and messed up. They carried me for a while until I got my head straightened out, but it didn't happen right away.

Looking back, the one thing that I know for sure is that being unhappy totally sucks. I learned that being in *the Rut* is no way to live, and I will never allow myself to go there again. I also know that no one except me could ever get me out. If you're in it, or know somebody who needs a hand getting out, think about these options:

■ Spend more time with your kids.

■ Spend more time doing stuff you really enjoy.

■ Go to a credit counselor.

■ Get additional training (and make yourself more valuable).

■ Try AA or rehab if it's booze or drugs.

■ Change your company or career entirely.

■ See a counselor or psychologist (hey if Tony Soprano can, so can you).

■ Start working out.

■ Volunteer at your church, or coach at your kids' school.

■ Get your GED, or take a class at a local junior college.

■ Get a really good lawyer if it's divorce or some other legal problem.

■ Run for Business Agent (now you're really asking for it).

■ Get a dog (or a hamster…smaller shits to clean up).

The major problem with being in *the Rut* is that you're not motivated to do much anyway. It's even harder to try something new. But that is exactly what you *must* do. You have to break the pattern. Otherwise, you'll just keep getting dragged down further. You have to get back in into action. Don't let it take one more minute from your life. You're worth more than that. You deserve to feel better.

It's a GOOD Life

No matter what happens, always remember that life is good. Sometimes it doesn't look that way, but if you think about it long enough, you'll see that it is pretty good. Being a union construction guy in North America is pretty damned awesome considering the alternatives. But you've got to get outside yourself for a minute to see it.

You're a guy with a job and profession to be proud of. You have a wage-and-fringe package worth between $35 and $50 per hour. You have health benefits, a pension, and maybe health care for when you get old. You'll be able to give your kids a good education if they want it. Everywhere you go you can see places you helped build with pride. That's just for starters. You've probably got all sorts of good things going on in your life. It's just hard not to take them for granted sometimes, that's all.

For comparison's sake, let's take a quick look at some of the other six billion people on the planet Earth:

■ Two billion of them can't read or write

■ Two and a half billion go to bed hungry every night

■ Three billion have dirt floors in their homes or no homes at all

■ Five billion have no savings, no insurance, no access to modern medicine.

That's *billion*, with a "b." I know what some of you are going to say: *Who cares? I don't know any people like that. I only see them on TV*. The point is, you're living pretty large. A hell of a lot better than about 80 percent of the people on the planet. You might not have Donald Trump's cash, but look at the bright side: you don't have his hair problem either.

Look, I don't want to get all preachy here, but when you start worrying about your life or your job, just try to remember that it's still a pretty good life. Life is never going to be perfect. Happiness is an art. You get it by working for what you need and want, enjoying what you've got, and forgetting about the rest.

Chapter Sixteen

Final Exam— Your Choices

"Your life is the sum of all your choices."

—Albert Camus

Choices, Choices, Choices

This book cannot *make* you do anything. It's completely up to you. Whatever you get out of this book will show in the choices you make from this day forward. Some of the choices are big, and some are small. They're about you, your family, your money, your job, your union, your community, and most of all, your future.

The kind of life you live depends on the choices you make every day. Freedom of choice is a powerful thing. Pretty much everything in this book is within your power to choose. Between being well off or broke, happy or frustrated, proud or ashamed. It's your choice. Choose well for yourself, because you're worth it. You can make a bigger difference than you realize.

Only If It's Good For You

When you read the lessons and advice in this book, there's only one thing that really matters. It has to be good for *you*. It has to make sense to you. It has to make you happier. More wealthy. More productive. More valuable to yourself, your family, and your employer. It has to work for you. Nobody knows what's better for you than you.

Final Exam

If you've made it this far, for all these pages, I want to thank you for sticking with me. That alone says something about you. Now it's time for your final exam, and you will be graded. By the industry, by your union brothers and sisters, and by yourself. Here's the exam. To finish this book, please choose one of the following four options:

Option A: Ignore this book and don't make any effort or commitment. Use the pages in the job site Porto-San. Tell everybody what a bunch of bullshit it is. Don't let it bother you that you could have been an elite achiever and gold medal winner. Watch union market share continue to shrink. Be road kill and be proud of it.

Option B: Be a skeptic. Figure that some of this material makes sense and will work for you. Don't admit it, but start changing your own approach. Only when it begins to prove itself, start to influence others. Notice that work and life have gotten better, but still bitch about things just to keep in practice.

Option C: Put all of it to work for you. Lead the effort by example. Be the best worker on every job site. Demand excellence from everybody around you. No excuses for anyone or anything, ever. Enjoy the respect, the Harley, the cabin, and the ski boat that come with it. Leave the job every day with the satisfaction of knowing that *you are the best in the world.*

Option D: In the days and weeks ahead quietly begin to make a better life for you and your family. Don't make a big deal about it, but make sure that you have your values, priorities, and life going in the right direction. Then pass this book along to somebody else you know who needs it.

And no matter what, have a great life.

Mark Breslin is the fourth generation of a construction family. His great grandfather, grandfather and stepfather were all contractors.

He has served as the Executive Director of the Engineering and Utility

Contractors Association for nearly 20 years. The association is a multi-employer bargaining organization that represents union construction firms in California doing billions of dollars in contracts each year. Mark became the chief executive and director at age 26. He has served in this capacity as chief negotiator and contractor advocate.

As a professional speaker, trainer and facilitator he has spoken to more than 50,000 business and labor leaders around the United States and Canada. He is the leading speaker in the nation on business development and marketing strategies for labor and management.

He graduated from San Francisco State University with a BA in Industrial Design. He has since taught labor relations and human resource management at Golden Gate and Sonoma State Universities.

Mark lives in northern California with his wife Susan and their three children. His real life passions include mountaineering and expedition travel. Recent challenges include summiting Mt. Rainier, trekking in the Sahara, and raising teenagers.

Breslin Strategies Tools & Resources

Organize or Die: A comprehensive "how-to" for professional organizing, business development and communications for labor and management.

Organize or Die Audio CD: Make use of your drive time with the new 2-CD set of Mark Breslin's Organize or Die. Gain the valuable lessons from this popular book of business strategy on this 2.5 hour audio program read by the author.

Survival of the Fittest: A call-to-action for the rank and file. A curriculum for apprentices and journeymen on the vital skills, attitudes and behaviors necessary to compete and win.

Survival of the Fittest Audio CD (2 CD set) Rank & file members spend hours on the road every day. How about using some of it to upgrade attitudes and behaviors. This 2-CD set, read by the author, is amusing, provoking and inspiring.

Survival of the Fittest Workbook and Discussion Guide brings the lessons home in a high-impact manner. Formatted so that every page requires student interaction, it is designed to provoke and stimulate training student discussions on subjects as varied as market share, absenteeism, harassment, integrity, competition, supervision, money management and more.

Survival of the Fittest Apprentice and Training Instructor's Guide for use by JACs and JATCs regionally and nationally. This guide takes an instructor, coordinator or training director step by step through the entire curriculum of *Survival of the Fittest*. It includes answer keys, role playing exercises and teaching formats. It is an essential companion to the student book and workbook.

Survival of the Fittest DVD: This DVD captures Mark Breslin's message of change and focuses on rank and file skills, behaviors and attitudes.

Survival of the Fittest Training Pack: A complete curriculum for evaluation including book, workbook, instructor's guide and DVD sampling. Mark Breslin's message on attitudes and behaviors.

Rank & File Education Series: The Breslin Business Plan

DVD Program One: Labor & Management Reality Check—Our Product & Market.
DVD Program Two: Our Image & The Union Yes Promise. These interactive DVD programs are designed to educate the rank and file as to the challenges we face in the market and the solutions and responsibilities that must be embraced to meet them. Can be used as support materials for the *Survival of the Fittest* curriculum. (2) 25 min. programs on one DVD.

Leading Edge Training
FOR TOP DOWN
ORGANIZING

Breslin
STRATEGIES INC.

Marketing & Business Development Kit
Strategic Tools & Training for Labor-Management Market Share

Includes • A Turn-Key Marketing, Sales and Training Package • 1.5 hours of Interactive Training • 70 Key Benefits and Talking Points • Custom Business Proposal • Introduction Letter Templates (5) • Phone Scripts • Testimonial Letter Templates (5) • Presentation Planning Outline • 25 Sample FAQs • 40 pages of Sample Documents in MS Word • User's Guide

The Breslin Strategies method of market share recovery has been proven in action in every market in the United States and Canada. Transforming an industry requires transforming individuals. The Marketing & Business Development Kit is designed to

- Boost confidence and performance
- Provide new skills and upgrade existing ones
- Increase job satisfaction and commitment
- Upgrade communication and correspondence
- Refine professional presentations
- Obtain commitments
- Drive results and increase market share

With thousands of new contracts signed, measurable increases in even the roughest markets and a more competitive playing field for contractors, unions and the rank and file, this program opens the door for our industry.

COMING IN 2008

Mark Breslin's newest book addresses the Alpha Dogs in the industry—the problem solvers who:

- Thrive on Achievement
- Hard-wired for Challenge
- Competitive to the Extreme
- Courageous and Risk Taking
- Bold, Assertive and Confident
- Results Oriented

An Alpha Dog is the person who "tends to assume a dominant role in social or professional situations, or thought to possess the qualities and confidence for leadership." That can be YOU!

ORDER YOUR COPY NOW!
USE THE ORDER FORM ON THE NEXT PAGE.

Improve Individual and Organizational Performance

CHECK **www.breslin.biz** OR ORDER HERE

Quantity	Title	Price ea.	Sales tax–Calif residents only	TOTAL DUE
	ORGANIZING AND MARKET SHARE			
	Organize or Die	$19.95	1.66 ea.	
	Organize or Die audio CD (2-CD set, 2.5 hrs)	$34.95	2.90 ea.	
	Marketing & Business Development Kit	$499.00	41.42 ea.	
	APPRENTICESHIP AND RANK & FILE: materials and media			
	Survival of the Fittest (book)	$19.95	1.66 ea.	
	Survival of the Fittest Workbook and Discussion Guide	$9.95	.83 ea.	
	Survival of the Fittest Apprentice and Training Instructor's Guide	$29.95	2.49 ea.	
	Survival of the Fittest Training Pack (book, workbook, instructor's guide, and DVD sampling, plus the Rank & File Education Series DVDs)	$393.00	32.62 ea.	
	Survival of the Fittest audio CD (2-CD set)	$24.95	2.07 ea.	
	Survival of the Fittest DVD	$149.95	12.45 ea.	
	Rank & File Education Series: The Breslin Business Plan DVDs (2)	$249.00	20.67 ea.	
	NEW: Alpha Dogs (DVD)	$249.00	20.67 ea.	
	COMING IN 2008: Alpha Dogs (book)	$19.95	1.66 ea.	
	NEW: Million Dollar Blue Collar (book)	$19.95	1.66 ea.	
	SHIPPING: $2.95 per item _____ items x $2.95 =			
	TOTAL:			

*FREE SHIPPING when ordering 50 items or more.

Canadian orders must be accompanied by a postal money order in U.S. funds. Allow 15 days for delivery.

Quantity discounts available • Call 866-351-6275

My check or money order for $_____ is enclosed.

Name_____ Phone _____

Organization_____ E-mail _____

Address _____

City/State/Zip _____

Please make your check payable & return to: **Breslin Strategies, Inc.**
c/o McAlly International Press
2415 San Ramon Valley Blvd, #4-230 • San Ramon, CA 94583

or to charge your purchase visit **www.breslin.biz**
or call **866-351-6275** • *fax* 925-829-9722